# Spiritual Slimming

Slim your life/Slim your body

Printed by Digital Book Print

# Spiritual Slimming

Slim your life/Slim your body

## Lara Wells

BOOKS

Winchester, UK
Washington, USA

First published by O-Books, 2010
O Books is an imprint of John Hunt Publishing Ltd., The Bothy, Deershot Lodge, Park Lane, Ropley,
Hants, SO24 0BE, UK
office1@o-books.net
www.o-books.com

For distributor details and how to order please visit the 'Ordering' section on our website.

Text copyright: Lara Wells 2008

ISBN: 978 1 84694 323 2

A CIP catalogue record for this book is available from the British Library.

Design: Stuart Davies

Printed in the UK by CPI Antony Rowe
Printed in the USA by Offset Paperback Mfrs, Inc

We operate a distinctive and ethical publishing philosophy in all
areas of our business, from our global network of authors to
production and worldwide distribution.

# CONTENTS

# INTRODUCTION

Being a medium was something that I didn't really plan on becoming. At school when the Careers people were working out my 'options', the computer said (NO!) I was told I was destined to be a Forensic Scientist. Actually they weren't really far wrong with that were they? The difference being I talk to dead people instead of dealing with the bodies of the dead people.

Over the years I have learned so much. As I realised my gift, I developed in other ways too. In between my very varied work as a medium, I worked as a motivator for a well known slimming company and I came to understand that the more weight that people had to lose, the more 'baggage' they had had to deal with in life.

The greatest fascination for me has to be people and I am blessed with meeting so many different people from different walks of life all with different personalities and lifestyles. As time progressed and my talent was honed, I began to find ways of 'blending' my energy with theirs and discovered that I could manipulate their energy by forcing my energy in a certain direction. For example, if you put a hyperactive child in a room full of calm children, you will notice that within minutes, the calm children will resonate their energy to 'blend' with the hyperactive child's and the hyperactive child will come down a few notches to balance with the calm children. We adults work in the same way. The saying 'like unto like' is particularly true in this instance. We are drawn to the people most alike ourselves in energy. The drop outs find each other, the musical people hang out together, scientific people group together and so on and so forth.

It's the energy within a person that dictates their friends and many a time (you've probably done this yourself if you are a parent) we will hear ourselves say the words that you promise

you never will utter

'Why can't you be more like so and so or who are you hanging out with because they are having a bad influence on you'

Yet, it's the energy within an individual that cause the attraction to take place. The vibrational level of that energy is dependant upon certain factors though and we will discuss more of this later in this book.

So, having established that we all are energy and if you take into account that scientists have proven that nothing can just cease to exist then you have a strong argument of the eternal question of life after death and is there such a thing. This book has not been written to address this eternal topic. But to understand that we should be aware of our ability to use this energy to balance, slim, motivate and, if fact, be the best we each of us can be. If you are reading this, then congratulations! You have taken the first step to shedding the baggage you have gathered over the years. It means that you 'want' to do something about where you are, how you feel and how you look. That baggage has been weighing you down. The vibration of your energy has slowed to produce a heavy feeling and your body will reciprocate to show you how your mind feels-**heavy!**

There are a number of things that can contribute to this and more to the point there is something you can do about it. So cast aside your reservations and that cynical mind and grace me with your attention for the duration of this book. Let me 'help you be all you can be' and your body will reward to you with the results.

*Thank you*
*Lara x*

# CHAPTER ONE

# WHAT MAKES US WHO WE ARE

*Gluttony is an emotional escape, a sign something is eating us.*
(Peter De Vries)

Strange how life turns out isn't it? There I am one minute about to give birth to my third son looking at an advert for a motivational slimming manager saying to my mum 'I can do that' and mentally telling myself that that was my job, and the next minute I am standing in front of my first class of what looked like a sea of people, perspiring profusely at the fear of delivering my first talk. I had taken my first step to conquering my nerves. It is not easy delivering talks to motivate hundreds of people on a weekly basis and I had put myself in the position of doing just that. Not bad for a girl who beat hundred of applicants to be where she dreaded to be. Basically I am quite shy and up until I had my first son, I wouldn't say 'boo' to a goose. But on reflection now, I have a lot to thank those classes for as they gave me my 'mojo' if you want to call it that and I am eternally grateful for the confidence, knowledge and people I met as a result of my time there.

In life we really do learn masses and everything counts towards the end result. You just don't see it as that at the time, do you?

My work and popularity developed at a remarkable rate, as did my mediumship and my fascination of why some people gain weight and not others drew me in to some really awesome arguments. Come on, you are bound to have been there. The cabbage soup diet, the Atkins diet, the grapefruit diet, the banana diet, the seafood and eat it diet – in fact, every diet ends with that dreaded word (diet) which in my book meant more like

**die** if you try-it! It's an awful word and someone should shoot the person who invented it. (only kidding so put your guns away and save them for later people)

Fortunately, most of us see the light and will swing towards a healthy eating plan so get into good habits. Notice the word 'plan' here as it is key to a chapter later in this book so keep reading.

The problem with a healthy heating plan is that it involves the word 'eating' and anyone out there who loves their food will probably make that the green light for eating everything in sight. Healthy does cause a slight panic for if we see the eating word first we indulge and then the healthy word (which to the mind has tagged itself along behind the word 'eating') and we immediately feel guilty and our emotions plummet and the devastation sinks in as we realise that after the eating we are no longer healthy!

Much has been written about food being up there with the word addictions and people are now starting to believe that along with alcohol, drugs and certain other vices, food is now classed officially as a addiction. Food is now 'Bad' once again and we indulge in a never- ending pledge of 'diet' or 'healthy eating' in a desperate attempt to get it under control (as if it has been let out of a cage) and in some sort of order in life.

You only have to glance at the many, many, magazines that grace our newsagent's shelves not to mention the front pages of most media types and the escapades of the WAGS to understand that looking good is now in fact a career option. Sad even though it is, I feel this is something to do with perfecting our lives and the unobtainable standards we put on ourselves. (Ms Pankhurst, we know you meant well but you have a lot to answer for!)

As I munched my way through kit kat after kit kat and flicked through the pages of them all, I admit, part of me wondered why I wasn't like that. Why did I have such little regard for how I looked? Was it body dysmorphia in reverse (I thought I looked better than I did) as I hated how I looked in pictures and avoided going to the swimming pool with the children, did I subconsciously think I wasn't worth all the effort into looking after myself? Then it hit me. I was rebelling! As I had been dealing with everyone else's grief and sorrows, I neglected to deal with my own. My body was bulking up to protect me emotionally. Now don't get me wrong, I have learned loads and I have never ever been what you call skinny. What I did discover was that when you are bigger, people think you are 'thick'. They treat you with contempt and think there is no grain of intelligence nestling in the loft area of oneself as how can there be if you allowed yourself to get physically in the state you are in? I found that I learned how to stand up for myself though and I became more than capable of surprising people with how much I knew. Since I had worked in the slimming industry, but had left before I actually discovered this I set about working out the vicious circle that people allow themselves to get into.

Along the way my reputation as a medium superseded me and my success as a thriving busy medium grew until I won the award in 2008 for 'Most Popular Spiritual Female-Psychic/Medium in the UK' voted for by the public, probably my clients. I worked hard to get there focusing only on helping others and bringing a glimmer of joy and closure into their lives after, often, very tragic events. It has been an incredible journey and privilege working with them all and I could never have come as far without their faith in me and spirits' faith in me.

All the late nights, working and driving each week 4-5 nights not getting in until 4-5 am each morning, dealing with grief and helping people get to where they need to be in life, I used food to get the energy to do this. Emotionally I was like a wrung out rag yet professionally after filming 2 TV programmes, appearing in multiple magazine and newspaper articles and travelling and touring all over the country I realised that something had to give. If I didn't pay attention to what my vibrational level was telling me then I would make myself ill. I had asked too much of it already and the time had come to support it instead of working against it. There is so much pressure in society to do well that we are very guilty of doing more than we should and we wonder why we make ourselves ill. So, ok I had been through the mill a bit. If I hadn't would I have been so effective in being the medium that I am. We are defined by what we experience in life aren't we so would I have changed anything? It's always a difficult one this isn't it?

The trouble is that we are brought up to believe that focusing on oneself is a somewhat selfish act and one that comes down on the list of priorities. Is it possible to be selfish and be good at what we do in this industry?

The answer lies in the positive and negative conditioning of the brain. As Freud lay ill in bed and just before he died, he allegedly wrote a letter to a good friend saying that for years he studied the conscious mind but realised that the answer to the mysteries of life, lay in the subconscious mind and how he wished he had his time over again as this is what he would have studied. How true that has proven to be. We know that the subconscious mind is larger than the conscious mind but we are unsure of its capacity. We know that the blueprint or template of what kind of partner we end up with in life is actually 'set' before the age of 5 which is why we tend to end up with a lifelong partner like our mum or dad as generally these are the people we have the most and first contact with up until that age. Scary isn't it?!

So, if that is the case, then there is possibly more in the subconscious mind than we think and then you compound that with all that you have gathered over the years and you take a good look at yourself and wonder why you end up the kind of person you are now? Hmm, yep... you have got it!

When you go on a path of self discovery to figure out why you are the person you are it takes you on many a weird route. I took to reading book upon book, listening to self- improvement programmes and speakers who were diverse. I made sure they all were on different subjects as I was careful not to have their interpretation affect my own. I read books on the law of attraction, books on channelling, books on healing and books on cosmic ordering and none of them told you exactly how to put into action all the explanations and theories they seemed so intent on brandishing about-a bit disappointing because I am a Taurus and I like practical!

Just how do you ask for what you want and when they talk about alignment, how do you do that exactly?

If you are wondering why I have digressed into an area of how to get what you ask for, it's because it is the same thing. The same alignment that gives you what you want can give you the size of body that you want as once you are in alignment with the energy around you, you are in harmony with the universal energy. If your energy vibrational level within your body is out of balance with the energy around you then all sorts of things can happen including health problems. The state of the mind has a direct reflection on the state of the body. The spirit is the energy within and this energy can stay within or travel out-with the physical self. Hence the saying, Mind, Spirit and Body. All of them connect and all have an impact on the other. Balance is the key and its in getting the balance that we can achieve not only the body we want, but the life we want as well. Balance is alignment and once this alignment is achieved, anything is possible and I mean anything. I have gone from homeless twice and the verge of bankruptcy to having a very comfortable lifestyle, providing for my 5 children who are extremely talented, who all play at least 2 musical instruments (one of them 4 instruments) have motivated the one son that they all wrote off, couldn't speak or hear properly let alone concentrate and is now doing fantastically well and continues to do so, am the main earner in my family with a fantastic standard of living, 2 cars, 3 businesses, winning a major award, having my work published and being one of THE most successful Spiritual Life Coaches in the UK today. Some of you may think that I have spoken materialistically but these are subconscious beliefs of someone who thinks money is nasty and only the really horrible people get somewhere. You need money to live on. I have tried to live without and I came unstuck and made it far harder on myself as a result. Today, I do not feel guilty about earning a good wage for what I do. Surely it is a reflection of your worth and if you are reading this right now and doing a job that you love in this industry and are poorer for it perhaps you are like I used to be and are putting others before your own needs which is commendable but doesn't keep the roof over your heads, does it? Then you need to take on board everything that is in this book for it is not really a book on slimming your body but in getting the control back in your life, dumping the baggage and bringing alignment and harmony to your world. This alignment will bring all sorts of changes. Some will be fantastic and you will go through some necessary and challenging changes. Like everything in life, it's about choice. To have a choice you have to have at least two things to choose from in life. How respectful are you to yourself when you limit your choice to being just what you have always done? The saying goes, 'If you do what you always do, then you will always get what you've always got.'

A client of mine had had a really rough few years. Not only did she 'die' for some 40 seconds on New Years' eve five years ago after being hit by a car, but she was told she would never walk again and would have severe memory problems. She did, in fact, walk again, after a lot of hard work and perseverance and when I met her some 2 years ago and after 2-3 consultations, she got the confidence and drive to set up her own business, and now has a Mercedes convertible and her own house bought and paid for by herself. I had the privilege of being part of that but something eluded her. A man to love her for who she was, and not what she had. Now, Susan had no problems in the looks department. She had gorgeous dark hair and brilliant blue eyes and brown skin so no this, was not an issue. The issue was that she kept being attracted to policemen. Through my coaching sessions we discovered that after she had been knocked down, the first person on the scene as she lay on the road was a police officer on his way home after just coming off duty and Suzy flitted in and out of conciousness. She, as a result of that awful situation, had a misplaced feeling of emotion towards every policeman she came into contact with and it was getting her into serious trouble I can tell you!

Now, Suzy was a determined woman that could focus on whatever she put her mind to. But by channelling her energies into her business and getting her home in tip top shape, she had forgotten about her own needs and was lonely. So, we set about having a plan for attracting the 'right' man to her rather than her being attracted to the type of man she thought she needed-totally a different thing. Here she made a choice and it turned out to be empowering for her indeed.

I was working on my newspaper in the area she lived in and we ended up in the same place one night and she offered to give me a lift back to my car. It was summertime and the nights were really light. So, we had a quick chat and a laugh and I got in the car. The conversation very quickly turned to the relationship side of things and she asked me where I would meet the love of her life I made a joke at which we both laughed and I then said,

'You know, Suzy knowing you, your car will break down and the right man will just come along to fix the car!' and we laughed some more.

Suddenly there was a burning smell and the black smoke shot out from the bonnet and we pulled over. We both sat in silence until we finally turned to look at each other and laughed out loud (thankfully!) and I then couldn't help but say

'Wouldn't it be really funny if the right man just happened to come along right' and we fell about with such rapturous laughter that any motorists passing by must've thought we were absolute crackpots!

Eventually, we climbed out of the car and Suzy pulled the bonnet open and out belched the smoke. I looked up and a van was coming towards us and high on all my laughter I screamed

'Ahhh, look out Suzy here is the man of your dreams right now!' and sure as my hair is red, the van pulled over and out stepped a dark haired man, in his early thirties with bulging biceps and overalls. He strode right up to Suzy and asked if he could help. The electrical energy passed between them and we found ourselves in the car with a lift home and he promptly gave Suzy his number. (and no, I'm am not making this up, this really did happen) Guess what? Yep, they are happily living together with plans for marriage and more importantly, no more policemen! Celebration or what!

Why did the sessions work? Because Suzy had to make a choice and then stick with it and she couldn't make this choice until she understood why she kept making the same mistakes over and over again. She was repeating a cycle and all cycles if they are causing unhappiness or angst in any way should be looked at and steps must be taken to break them. That's when the magic began. That day, we fine-tuned her energy vibration and it automatically pulled in the man that was on that frequency (we will look at this more in depth with my next book 'Spiritual Slimming for Love') and so by looking at this case, we begin to get an idea that there is truth in the whole vibration thing. Our choices are important as they shape our lives yet we often barely think about this and automatically act upon familiarity. It is indeed a privilege to be able to have a choice never mind make one yet we persistently act like it is a bad thing. Surely if we go against the natural flow of life, we are creating resistance and this has a negative effect as its like trying to drive forward when the car is in reverse. The result is that you will get nowhere FAST! When you are going forward to decide on which road to take and you never drive along the same road forever do you? Then surely your life should be regarded in the same manner shouldn't it?

This can be applied to so many areas of your life but for now, think about the word 'Choice'- what do you choose?

You are about to get into your own personal car. Now, start the engine and put it in the gear to go forward. Smile and put your foot on the accelerator as you drive with me through the road ahead. There will be roads off this one and each time you get to one of those roads you will have to decide on whether to turn in or not. You see, it's about choice and the fun is in the choosing.

Drive with me as we take this incredible journey together. Miracles can happen along the way you know....

*"I shall shape my future. Whether I fail or succeed shall be no man's doing but my own. I am the force; I can clear any obstacle before me. Or I can be lost in the maze. My choice. My responsibility. Win or lose, only I hold the key to my destiny."*
(Anon)

# CHAPTER TWO

# HOW DO YOU WORK?

*When you expect success, your mind focuses on success.*

First things first, how do you work? If we get an understanding of this then we can begin. When I see a client, I make it a priority to understand them. All anyone wants is to be understood and for people to 'get' them. I am a psychic and medium. The word 'medium' actually means 'communicator' and to communicate effectively is indeed an extraordinary gift. My speciality is to understand the person and its not what they often say but in what they don't say. The following questions I will put to them on the initial session. It helps me communicate on a verbal level but trust me, the initial communication has already happened with my energy blending with theirs. As I deepen the communication, I watch for body language, eye contact and facial expressions that sometimes help to explain things further. I will notice whether they flinch or sometimes distance themselves or avoid answering directly and above all, I will know if they lie or fabricate in any way. My job, in other words, is to see beyond what I visually see as often this is the answer of why they have allowed themselves to get to this stage in the first place. As you are reading this book, I am assuming that you would also like to understand yourself better. This is good as you have acknowledged that you are constantly learning about you and evolving.

## STAGE 1
### First of all ask these questions:

What do you do for a living?

What hours do you work?

Do you like your work?

In your opinion, do you eat healthily?

What are your energy levels like?

How is your general health?

Do you have financial worries?

What is the one thing that stands out for you that you have done or experienced in the past?

What kind of background do you come from?

Your relationship with your parents-how is it?

How is your love life?

Your love life in the past- how was that and how did it end?

Other types of relationships, friendships etc, how do you find those?

How do you see life in general?

Do you think you are a negative or positive thinker?

Name something fantastic about yourself that you like.

## STAGE 2

How have you answered? Was it..

A)   How you felt?

B)   What you thought we wanted to hear?

C)   What you should've done but didn't?

D)   What your mother would've told you to do?

We are all fantastic at *knowing* what to do but actually *doing it* can be a whole different ball game.

**Now** answer them again and see whether you get the same answers. Make a big effort to put the **truth** and don't worry about what anyone else will think. Now is the time to be honest.

This is a bit like writing. None of us authors get it right the first draft. We have to write it a number of times. This is called 'Layer Stripping' and what I am doing is stripping back the layers that life has put on you as a result of emotional deprivation.

Recently, I had an evening of private consultations at home. Each client saw me individually and didn't know each other. The first woman, a lovely looking girl, had a husband that was cheating on her, the second woman had a husband who was cheating on her too. The third woman (at the risk of sounding like goldielocks and the three bears) was also married but with two children, she had gorgeous dark glossy hair, a full face of make up, was immaculately dressed and (you've guessed it) was having his third affair! Well, by that time, I had to admit, I was becoming slightly unhinged myself and it made me sit right back and ask myself why this was happening. Could the problem be arising from the women themselves? I looked into my third clients' eyes and I saw something quite startling. Her eyes appeared to have no shine in them at all. I sat back and it hit me like a thunderbolt (well, I do have some psychic moments you know!) and I started to see pictures in my mind of a father that had walked out on her when she was a young child, a mother who was emotionally challenged and trailed one man after another home and my client looking scared and lost. I looked her up and down. She was stunning. A little bit overweight, but that was understandable, and her make-up now almost too perfect. It was layered, rather like an onion. Now you and I both know that onions come in different sizes depending on the amount of layers. You will notice that each onion you are taught to take the gold coloured skin off as well as the tough layers on the external surface. People are the same. We all have the tough layers on the outside (for some women the make-up and the trowel jokes have grown from that!) however, once we cut those away, we can get to the real issues and the sensitive, softer part. Our bodies mirror this also. The bigger people have produced more tough layers as protection to the soft, sensitive side (now you are probably getting it) We still have to want to do that but successful weight loss is about more than just losing weight. We have to keep it off and that means addressing the problems that put it all there to begin with. So, how you feel is important and how you feel affects the vibration (a frequency of energy given off by the body which reflects the emotional status) We have to help your mind get rid of what is weighing it down. This will raise your vibrational level and increase your energy level in turn. The mind and body will come into alignment and your body will shed its protective layers to mirror the mind. Light of mind equals light of body. We all have the ability and power to do this. We just have to *decide*, and **THEN** we have to take *action*.

*"The higher your energy level, the more efficient your body. The more efficient your body, the better you feel and the more you will use your talent to produce outstanding results.*
Anthony Robbins

Emotional deprivation leads to layering. The tough outer layer wears make-up. Take that off and it is soft and sensitive. My client was hiding a fear of being a failure and her husband knew this and used it to his advantage. She also admitted to feeling worthless and unlovable so I recommended some coaching sessions and she decided to (not surprisingly) leave her husband and is getting to know herself a bit better before she jumps headlong into another relationship again. One day at a time. Interestingly, I noticed on our last session, that although she maintains that she is not trying to lose weight, she has slimmed down a bit and is looking fabulous!

My client was emotionally unsure of love as she grew up and as a result had not developed the necessary survival skills required for a relationship. She became clingy and needy and her husband used this to his advantage. Before you all think that I dislike this man, it does take two for the breakdown of a relationship. This man did have his own issues, however, he wasn't my client so could do nothing for him. I understand that his own father had affairs which is sad as he too was pre-programmed for this type of life and walked into this without thought. The two of them remain friends for the children and are getting on better than they did when together which is good for the children.

Oh, stop press! Have just had a phone call from her would you believe, she has enrolled on the course that she wanted to do-fantastic!

So, now we have acknowledged all that has brought you to this point in your own lives, we have to understand that we are all made up of 'moments'. The more 'moments' we experience, the more they stack up. This is a bit like a wall built with bricks. A house is built with bricks. We build our bodies in the same way. But like we can move house, we can re-assemble our bodies so we feel like we are in a new house. Stage three will help you to pick those new bricks.

## STAGE 3

1.  Is it a new size of clothes you want or a target weight?
2.  Do you want to have good health?
3.  Write three things that you feel will improve if you were to balance your mind and your body together to be in alignment.
4.  How do you think that will make you feel?
5.  What's stopping you?
6.  Realise there is no right time only the here and now. Begin now.
7.  Understand that the mind is not in control but a tool that if

you use correctly can work **for** you. Do you feel that your mind works **for** you or **against** you?

8. Do you feel compelled to help people?

9. Do you want to be in a place that will take you to enrich your life?

10. Draw a picture of how you look now (the house you live in now) and then one of how your house will look afterwards. If it helps, cut them out of magazines. Use one of you now and one from a magazine for after if you like. Be funny and put your head on top.

Understand that it has taken time to get to where you are now in life and it will take time to undo that. Let's not forget that **YOU** are important. To help others you have to help **YOU** first then when you are in a good place, you can help them. Understand that as our habits have developed unconsciously, we have to consciously make a plan for routine and habits and this will then allow us to work on what we have developed subconsciously. After all, if we were to have a house built, would we just throw the bricks down and hope that it erects itself to something that we want or would we employ an architect to design our house properly, obtain the permission necessary and build it to require-ments? Of course we would. Then treat your body with the same respect.

I have to say that I had spent so long in helping others that I made the fatal mistake of neglecting myself in the process. Over the years I gained a fantastic reputation but had lost who I was and where I was going. I'll bet there are a few of you reading this right now who have felt the same or are feeling like this right now. I was giving more and more until I was working 20 hour days with very little sleep and still getting up with the children and doing the school run and the whole day would start all over again. Crazy, I know, but when the demand on your ability is there and people are reliant on you, you do feel like you have to pull out all the stops and be there for them. I am often the last port of call and what if the person I turned away was the one that needed the most help?

Before you judge me, remember that despite my many challenges I actually haven't had a cold for over fourteen years and I was and am in great health. But, the weight went on, and on and on. My metabolism had shut down due to massive amounts of stress hormones released into my system and my body started layering to protect me. I was driving hundreds and hundreds of miles weekly and my own body decided that as it was receiving the signals that I was under pressure and internalising sometimes massive problems, I had to have the resources to deal with it and it didn't let me down!

Then one day, as I was taking my anti-depressant I thought 'I've had enough!' and decided to take action and look into why this was happening and decided that I wasn't actually happy and I was burying myself in other people's problems to avoid what was making me unhappy at home. I had to restructure my life and get some organisation going and decide how much I was going to do and when. But first of all, I had to take a step back and take a long hard look at things and allow my mind to digest what was going on.

First of all, the loss of the people close to me had to be taken on board and come to terms with. The cold hard facts were that due to my work, people were unrelenting on me and didn't seem to understand that death still has the same psychological impact on us mediums even though we know there is an afterlife, we still have to adjust to the physical loss like everyone else.

And that is what I did. I took time out and was just 'Lara' mother and housewife. I found my own 'power' as it were and discovered that I didn't really have friends as such but people who just wanted me for what I could do. So, I got me some friends who were different. Friends, who had a completely different professional status and would talk about things non-relating to my work, which most definitely worked a treat. Over time, my confidence grew. My children began to get a social life and I made the effort to invite people over more and the balance began to shift. I felt happier as the 'other' side of my personality was getting a much- needed chance to breath.

I am not going to lie to you and say it was easy. In between having children, juggling a relationship and seeing to the home as well as managing 2 children with attention deficit disorder, life inevitably got complicated. There is a lot written about the ego and stripping it back to work from the heart. However, without the ego to drive you, you are in danger of being hollow.

I have read and listened to others' account of the ego in their bid to be as spiritual as they can be. Compassion, understanding and experience will make you more spiritual. You have to have a 'drive' to help others. How can that be if there is no ego at all? People who are so wrapped up in washing away the ego are so wrapped up in themselves they see nothing else-is that spiritual?

By helping one person be the best they can be, you gain a certain satisfaction that compels you to help someone else and so on and so forth. Being intent on finding your own spiritual growth will only hold you back. Find the spiritual growth in others and your own will progress beyond all expectations and limits.

However, in order to do so, you have to be right in yourself. Take action and look to things that will harmonise the balance. If you are all work, find the play. Learn to laugh and above all, respect yourself.

**Respect for you** comes from life experience. Our respect for ourselves often comes way down the list of priorities and is a direct result of experience in life. Emotions affect the psychological and then the physical. To control your emotion is then the key to the psychological and will impact on how we respect our bodies.

## STAGE 4

1.  If something unexpected happened to you or someone you care about, how would you react?
2.  Do you think negatively at all?
3.  If so, how long for?
4.  Do you allow negative thoughts to rule your life?
5.  Do you admit to always looking on the 'darker' side of things that happen?
6.  In your opinion, do you think that you pre-anticipate bad things happening before they happen?
7.  Do you tend to cater for situations 'just in case?'
8.  Would you say you react to a poverty mindset (i.e. to having nothing or a fear of having nothing?)

Be as honest with yourself as you can when you answer these questions. Don't put what you think I want to hear but what is real to you after all if you can't be honest with yourself who can you be honest with?

Right, now we have that established, I want you to make a list of what you think is holding you back. Try and write 10 things and list them in order of importance.

*Keep your heart open to dreams. For as long as there's a dream, there is hope, and as long as there is hope, there is joy in living.*
(Anonymous)

# CHAPTER THREE

# LETS GET GOING

*Those who wish to sing will always find a song.*
(Swedish Proverb)

For years now we have been 'fed' information and strategies on how to lose weight. When I worked with racehorses between the ages of 16 and 19, I was taught that to lose weight I had to eat less. Well, that sent the blood sugars haywire and the moods all over the place. I saw my colleagues run around fields with bin liners to sweat the last bit of excess fluid to reach their riding weight or they would get thrown off the ride and substituted for another jockey. I saw them go days without eating and would often ride in the race feeling as weak as a kitten-very dangerous and putting hundreds of thousands of pounds of equine flesh and bones at risk too if they made one wrong move. The race riding world is corrupt that's for sure and everyone associated with it often ends up with 'shot' metabolisms and overweight in latter years. The one main essence of this is because of the feeling of being deprived. Did you answer 'yes' to this on your questionnaire?

Depravation in one way or form is probably the one key area of weight gain that we, as people, have. Before you get all shirty on this, it's not just food we are talking about here. The list I associate with is below. Do you associate with any of them?

1. Being deprived of Love
2. Being deprived of Money
3. Being deprived of security

4.  Being deprived of a secure job
5.  Being deprived of fundamental basics
6.  Being deprived of friends
7.  Being deprived of food whilst growing up
8.  Being deprived of a home
9.  Being deprived of a family
10. Being deprived of physical contact

If you related to some or all of these then the chances are this would manifest in some way as a negative emotional trait. Negative emotional traits are heavy and make your vibration slow down, a bit like carrying a rucksack. This slows the system/metabolism resulting in less calories being burned and weight starts to be retained.

Last year, I took a phone call from someone who was a patient at the mental institute. She asked if I would go and see her and read for her. I agreed. My mother thought I was 'mad' to entertain the very idea as I knew nothing about her and didn't know the situation I would be presented with. I knew that if I wasn't meant to go, then I would have missed her call and in my mind, everyone is equal and deserves the same rights as everyone else. If that was someone who lived in a house, would I see them? Of course I would. So, I packed my case and knocked and rang the door of the secure unit. I was to pretend I was a hairdresser as she didn't want the staff finding out what she was having done. Now, I laugh at this point because anyone who reads the paper would know who I was and would recognise me in an instant. However, I went along with it to keep her happy.

Sure enough, the door was answered and I said my name and that I was Claire's hairdresser. The nurse smiled and said,

'Hello Lara, we are expecting you.'

'Yes,' I replied. 'I knew you would be but just pretend you don't know me ok? It will keep her happy.'

'Of course.'

And in I walked, carrying my pink case filled with the tools of my trade.

I entered the room and my client sat on her chair. She asked that we be left alone.

I took a good look at her. Her eyes were dull, her hair washed but dull also. Her skin was a deathly pallor and she played with her fingers constantly. She also had a tube taped to her cheek that she was being fed through.

I set my table up then turned to face her square on.

'Claire, sweetheart, I know why you have got me to come here.'

'Oh, why?' she retorted aggressively

'You want me to tell you if you are going to be successful in killing yourself!'

Claire gasped and visibly looked taken aback

'How on earth did you know that?' she asked

'I can feel it from you so please don't pretend to tell me otherwise.'

I continued to tell her that she had been raped by her father and her mother to this day didn't know yet continued to visit her daughter every day and then some!

Her father eventually left her mother and Claire had had nothing to do with her father since then but it was still within her.

'You must tell your mother Claire. You are so angry because she hasn't noticed yet she must look at you now and wonder what has happened.'

'Yes, I know but I can't find the right time,' she said

She looked at me and I could see that she was far away as she contemplated this instruction.

Eventually, she looked at me and said

'You are right. I will tell her. You sure I am not going to die soon?'

'Claire I think if you were meant to go, you would've been gone before now. Lord knows you have had every opportunity to haven't you?'

'Yes. I still don't know how you knew all that. I didn't tell you a thing! Thank you for being so straight with me. I needed that'

And with that, I left. Three months later, I met Claire again in a shop. She had the tube out of her nose and she looked much happier than the last time I saw her. She told me she had told her mother. Her mother was very, very upset because she had thought it was her fault. Claire had recognised that she had been disappointed that her mother didn't notice the abuse and had held that against her. Her eating was back to normal and she felt that she wanted to live rather than die. I can't tell you how happy I felt myself that day when I bumped into her. By being upfront and treating her with respect, she saw that she still had respect for herself and her mum. There has been a lot of emotional baggage for this girl to deal with. She nearly buckled under the strain. Sometimes it is too much to bear and you feel like you are going under. When she could no longer bear it, she shut down and that included her eating. Her energy was trapped and couldn't move. Spiritually, she was deficit.

When I looked at her that day, I saw a little girl, smiling and free. Her spirit re-ignited, her energy flowing.

Now, everything has energy. It is not possible to just cease to exist. A good example of this process is if you boil water, it turns to steam and as the steam cools it condenses back to water again. Plants have energy, people have energy, animals have energy and this energy resonates at an individual rate. Science will tell you that each of us have molecules that vibrate. Energy vibrates also causing a reaction. The higher the vibration the more the vibration of your individual energy will react and this vibration determines many, many things. Mediums have the ability to vibrate their energy at a much higher rate than other people. The word 'Medium' simply means communicator. Could it be that we then communicate through this energy and if we do, then with what?

I have spent the last few years exploring this and have gone around various churches in the attempt to 'feel' a higher power in some way, shape or form that even matches or comes close to that of which I feel when I am connecting with spirit. When I connect with spirit I often use the term 'plugged in' as the energy I can feel from that makes a huge difference to how I feel, talk and work. When you plug a lamp in the electrical current is released into the wires through the metal conductors and the surge of electrical energy travels up the wires. This energy vibrates and will cause a bit of heat in the process. The covering to the wires are insulating to protect against a fire being caused by this heat. Once the electrical energy reaches the light bulb, the electrical vibration is higher and heat is then released into the glass bulb making light. This light is illuminating. The energy I feel when I am plugged in makes me feel illuminated also. Through this we can help our bodies to heal, feel and speak to spirit and harness the abundance we all need in life. We each are our own mediums. We all have the ability to make our energy vibrate high enough to do all this if we release it. Once released, this will bring us into alignment with the 'higher' power or 'universal' energy of which we are all connected. I know that as you are reading this book, you are prepared to take on board the whole concept of spiritual slimming but others around you will probably be a bit more sceptical. We each have our own life path and some of us evolve a bit sooner and further than others.

*Great spirits have always encountered violent opposition from mediocre minds.*
(Albert Einstein)

25

Albert Einstein was right when he said this quote. However, we can take this further and there is every reason that these mediocre minds can be freed to acknowledge the great spirit that is within each and every one of us to link with the even greater spirit around us.

Free your mind and the rest will follow. This is true in any aspect. How many of your worry about paying a bill or bills or finding the money for a project and you worry yourself sick about it don't you? Then at the last hour, you find the money and everything is ok and peace and harmony remains-until the next time!

What if I were to tell you to expect the money to pay the bills and sit back and wait for it to arrive-would you relax and be assured that it will happen?

But if you were to tackle it productively by taking action, you would be able to work your way around this no problem at all because you have been conditioned to only expect something if you have worked hard for it.

You see, when put like that, you begin to realise that the mind is actually imprisoned not only by the skull but by your thoughts. Your thoughts define who you are. If you really want to boil it right down though, look around you. Everything you see once started with someone's thought. A thought can create so much yet we give it little value. We tell ourselves that thoughts can be changed so they are fickle and have no weight to them. Sometimes lack of thought can change things also but we need to think to decide on not to think. How often has someone asked you when you are looking distant,

'What are you thinking?' only for you to reply

'Nothing'

Driving home recently, a strange thing happened. I had been at a good friends photo shoot for the cover of her new book. I had taken my cousin and we were having a right old chinwag. These were indeed exciting times as Joanne, who is an excellent communicator in the animal world, had been working so hard to get to where she was and I am truly proud of her.

On the way back, I normally followed my 'Satalite navigation' but this time, I was so busy chatting, I subconsciously took road that was different to the usual one to get onto the motorway.

As we were parked at the three-lane roundabout, I fell silent. On my right hand side was a massive article lorry which was the inside lane. I don't know if there was anything on the other side of him but when the traffic lights changed, He pulled off and I stayed where I was twirling my hair. My cousin said 'Lara the lights have changed' but I stayed put and out of nowhere the lorry then pulled right in front of us, narrowly missing the car by millimetres!

We watched in horror as the driver mounted the island, drove up the grass verge, roared right up into the air and ploughed through the car park and into the side of the restaurant. Luckily, the head waitress heard it coming and screamed for everyone to get out of the way. I drove around the roundabout and up to the car park (where we were eventually blocked in by the police tape) to see if the driver needed help. I just 'knew' he was dead from a heart attack though as I reasoned that I may not be able to pick up on a live person driving a 44 ton arctic lorry but next to me at the traffic lights, if a dead man was driving this lorry, I would pick up on it. Even though my cousin thought I was in a dream, part of my mind was thinking for if I had even just moved a few feet, I would've been killed, my cousin would've been killed not to mention the people in the three cars behind us.

It took me a few weeks before I could drive down that motorway again only to realise when I looked for the road that I couldn't find it and that was when I had to acknowledge that I had subconcously taken a different road that day.

I came away from that incident feeling so incredibly fortunate that I was going home to my family that night and the driver of the lorry, who I didn't know, wouldn't be. I was encouraged to think that there is definitely a bigger game plan and that every action derives from a single thought. That lorry driver must've felt something happen as he was heading to the roundabout in the first place. How did he maintain his position? That would've taken some immense strength. I am thankful for that and for the people he saved before he died. After that, it was up to divine chance-or was it?

No, I certainly won't be taking anything for granted again. We are all linked in one way, shape or form.

If I hadn't been in a good place myself that particular day, would it have turned out differently though?

What are you thankful for? Make a point of thinking and acknowledging whatever you are thankful for and spend time taking on board how you feel.

Remember that:

**Thought is Energy**

**When we think a thought, it is projected into the universe at a certain vibration.**

Understand that:

**'Thoughts are magnetic and attract the same vibration as the thought you have sent out'**

**With that in mind, the answer has to be to raise the vibration of each and every thought that you send out so that each time it is attracted back to you, it is magnified in intensity. You will illuminate as a result of this until only good things happen. Don't be afraid to ask with confidence. This will encourage you to be in a good place as you see the proof of your changes.**

After all, even the good book says **'ask and you shall receive'!**
**Now we know what that does actually mean.**

# CHAPTER FOUR

# WHAT FREQUENCY ARE YOU ON?

*Not to have control over the senses is like sailing in a rudderless ship, bound to break to pieces on coming in contact with the very first rock.*
(Gandhi)

I often meet with opposition in my job. People are proud. They seek help then will be angry with themselves for having to ask for help in the first place. We as a nation always are quick to judge. Instead of celebrating success, we are suspicious of it. Lets change that and make that change by changing how we think.

Further back in the book we discussed being deprived of something. This means we have felt that we have gone without at some point in our lives and because of this we have developed a fear. The jockeys I worked with in my early working years were deprived of food and fluid. This would lead to food issues later on. Many would resort to taking medication, legal or illegal and this also leads to implications. Fear is very delibitating and can make us develop a block that will hinder our success. To get rid of those fears we must get the message that we no longer are deprived. This is also a basic security within us all.

Many of us will run our every day life with these fears and put up with them not realising that they are, in fact, sabotaging our life by dragging us down and hindering our minds to be in alignment with our bodies.

I had a fear of being me. I spent so long focusing on making others happy and doing what was expected of me, and they liked and relied on me for doing just that. I had developed into a very curvy, mother figure as a result. Someone who was trustworthy and dependable and I ate to make sure I stayed like that. After all, I couldn't let them down now could I? I was afraid that no one would like me for me. I learned early on that people would be confrontational if you competed with them so I took myself out of the equation. In fact, even as far back as when I worked for my first racing yard, I was always more of the build to be a 'Jump Jockey' even at my slimmest. All the other girls were at least 2 stones lighter than me. However, I had a tiny waist and curvy hips and a bust and all the men made their intentions clear, even when I didn't want their advances. It's sad to say, that those unwanted passes were men who thought they could take sexually from me without asking as the racing world is very much a male dominated world even today. I couldn't even groom my horses without my male bosses coming into the stable and trying it on with me. I dreaded being on my own because they would be waiting to pounce. It was always made clear that I had to 'put out' if I were to get anywhere in the racing world or I wouldn't make it at all. I was a fantastic race rider and at the age of 17, on a job seekers wage, I was in charge of my own yard with 11 horses to look after. A lot of the horses were yearlings. However, this only made things harder for me as I became a sitting duck with those that wanted to make me a target for their sexual advances.

The boss's daughter was extremely well known and very glamorous. Unfortunately, because I had all the attributes for attracting men (not welcome ones as you would've gathered by now) she took an intense dislike to me, and I got the blame for anything that went wrong and was constantly taken off the riding out list.

The other girls, they were the same. Their boyfriends constantly threw themselves at me and eventually, they stopped inviting me along on their nights out. I still tried to make things work when disaster struck one Sunday evening, we were all so tired from travelling back from our mutual weekend off, that we failed to attend at the local pub where one of the boyfriend of one of the girls was waiting. We didn't show and he jumped on his push- bike (there were no mobile phones in those days) and proceeded to cycle home. David, sadly, was knocked off his bike, as he was cycling, by drunk- drivers and he hit his head in the danger place at the back of the skull and died. The paramedics resuscitated him and he was put on life support. Three days later, his life support was switched off. It was devastating and I supported everyone concerned through it all. They still chose to dislike me after things settled down and I remember feeling disheartened and disillusioned. To be honest, I then began to not care how I looked and women began to see me as less of a threat. I was finally accepted and since then, I have always refuse to compete where my appearance is concerned. Now, I know its not about appearance, but for the last twenty years, I have been on a rollercoaster where I was forced to examine my lack of respect for myself to the point that I was self-sabotaging my healthy eating. This derived from fear of rejection and had to be addressed. It took sometime and a total stripping back of all that I had 'learned' to get through this life-not necessarily to get on. I learned about survival, but not about living. I spent a huge proportion of my life being pregnant and although I would not sway my children for love nor money, I realise also, that this was another excuse to 'hide'.

Now, before you all go running off screaming, like I have said before, this is not a book about slimming. This is about dumping the baggage that is holding you back from being you. This allows your body to raise its vibrational level to connect with a higher universal power and then you can access unlimited requests, energy, happiness, financial expectations, true faith, under-standing and a leaner body. I know, because I did it. And continue to do it. This book is me giving you all a nudge and educating you in what I have learned. Giving you the benefit of my hard work and windy, trodden roads. My path now has flowers growing along it and I so want you to have flowers along yours too!

I can safely say, that to be a good medium before, I worked my socks off and pushed myself so hard. I gave it my all. Now when I 'connect' with spirit, I can do it so easily and marvel at the hard time I gave myself. Why did I make it so hard for me? Ah, yes. I chose that path a long time ago. I made it harder for myself to hide and be accepted and liked. Now, I can look good, be accepted and be liked as I have got rid of the fears that trapped my thinking. Face yourself, love thyself and you can truly love others unconditionally. Now, I also understand that if people don't accept me for me, it is their problem and not mine.

The questions I asked earlier will make you think more about how you got to be where you are today. There is always room for improvement and it is a fantastic day when you realise that the only consistency with all our lives and the only thing we are hear for is to learn, self improve and advance. If you don't do any or all of those 3 things then you are 'stuck' and there is little wonder why you are faced with the job you have on your hands now.

How you feel will determine what frequency you are on. If you feel a low dragging feeling, then you are on a low frequency. If you feel high and excitable, positive and vibrant, then you are on a high frequency.

**NOTE:**
Take note on how you feel before we do this next exercise.

**EXERCISE TO LIFT/REPLACE A FEAR**

1.  Sit in a quiet place.
2.  Look over the questions again that I asked earlier on in this book.
3.  Now look at the list of reasons that you would feel deprived

in some way, shape or form. Be honest!

*'Preconceived notions are the locks on the door to wisdom.'*
(Merry Browne)

4. Now feet on the floor (to ground you) close your eyes and put an image of what you consider to be a major factor in you feeling negative. Hold that image.
5. Breath in and out deeply letting your breath 'go' very slowly with control. As you blow out, imagine you are blowing away all the negativity and reasons that you found yourself in this place in life to begin with.
6. Now, think of something you are afraid of or intensely dislike and put that alongside the other image. Hold that thought and mentally note how you feel.
7. Do the breathing exercise again like before. At the same time, take your right hand and to the back of the left hand, pinch a bit of skin and twist it tightly. This will hurt and is designed to associate the nasty images with pain. Now, get up and put some music on that you just LOVE and turn the volume up to as loud as you can manage to stand it. Close you eyes and picture a happy memory. At the same time dance in time with the music and throw yourself around as if you were dancing like nobody were watching.
10. Laugh out loud and smile. Overdo it if you can and whoop with delight. In your mind or out loud ask for the perfect body. Ask for the weight loss you want/the goal you want/new job/money/relationship/house and see yourself already there- that's the stuff!

YOU **WILL** HAVE THAT BODY YOU DESERVE!
YOU **WILL** HAVE THE LIFE YOU DESERVE!
YOU **WILL** BE ALL YOU CAN BE AND **MORE**!

## How do you feel now?

Music does wonders for the soul and the vibrational level of an individual can change depending on the music played. What we are doing is association techniques. We are associating negative thoughts with pain and positive thoughts with laughter and music. This exercise should be repeated every day for 12 weeks. Why 12 weeks? Because studies carried out say we need 6 weeks to get rid of old and bad habits and 6 weeks to re-instil new and good ones so we will do this for 12 weeks to get the best effect!

Now, at the back of this book are some pages for you to write on. I want you at this point to write down your aims and your dreams of what you want your reality to be. We are going to use this as your very own **'Spiritual Slimming Wish Board'** and when you are writing this, you are in a happy place, are positive and believe that you are going to do this. Laugh at the same time if you want to or smile to yourself. This will align your higher vibrational frequency with that of the higher more positive vibrational frequency of the universal energy and as you do that you body is already on its way to becoming slimmer. Believe it, and it will believe!

Three days before mother's day two years ago, Jennifer's friend, Karen, called me to say her friend really needed to see me. She was extremely worried about her and I didn't hesitate to see her even though the only time I could was actually Mother's Day itself. I booked her in.

Mother's Day arrived and I was given yellow roses (my favourite) and chocolates. As I was cutting the roses to fit on the vase, a man's voice asked if I would save one for his wife.

'Who is your wife?' I asked hesitantly looking around me to see if I could see him.

'She is coming to see you soon,' said the voice.

I shrugged, puzzled on what he meant. The woman who had

booked the reading had made her friend sound young so I thought that he must've meant later in the week. However, I left one rose to the side just in case.

'What's your name,' I asked

'Cal' he said


I opened the door not sure of what to expect. Two well groomed women stood before me.

'This is Jennifer and I'm Karen' said the taller one.

I smiled and greeted them and welcomed them into my home. We trekked down the stairs to my waiting room where I sat Karen and instructed one of the children to get her a coffee. I seated Jennifer in my consultation room.

Not knowing what to expect, I exchanged a few words and tried to reassure her that she would be ok as it was her first time.

As soon as I went quiet, I could here the same man that had spoken to me earlier on that day. I took a long hard look at this woman before me. She couldn't have been more than thirty-seven. She confirmed that she was. She looked so young to have lost her...

'I have your husband here' I said quickly

'He said you have a bum to die for!'

She suddenly laughed out loud and then dissolved into tears.

'He says his name is Cal and he was with me earlier. He seemed to know you were coming.

'Yes, that is him. I told him I was coming and I prayed and prayed that he heard me.'

Reassured I carried on. He told me he was driving a lorry early in the morning. It was foggy and there was a crane at the side of the road. The long arm was positioned wrongly and the lorry due to the fog drifted too close to the crane. The crane arm decapitated the cabin of the lorry taking this fine young man with him. An horrendous way to go. He also told me his phone was missing and that he had two children a boy and a girl. His funeral was packed and filled the roads as they gave him good send off. Jennifer's husband had just turned forty-no age at all!

It was good to see Jennifer laugh at some of the passes he made at her. I could see her energy grow as she acknowledged the information relayed to her. As she left to go home, she thanked me.

'Just a minute, I have something for you,' I said as I ran off to get the Rose. 'Cal told me to give you this as they were your favourites. He also said he didn't forget it was Mother's day and to say Happy Mother's day!'

She gently took the rose from me and looked me square in the eyes.

'I will never forget what you have done for me today. You have made such a difference. I know I have a long way to go now but I now know he is right there with me.'

And with that agreed to keep in touch.

After that session, Jennifer did indeed keep coming to see me. We worked on healing her by using various exercises to increase the vibrational level. This helped her work through her depression, her fears and anxieties. She began to feel 'Cal' around her and was amazed at how much she picked up. After he died, she couldn't even bear to be in the house they shared so she moved to her mum's house. Six months later she felt confident enough to go in and re-decorate the entire house one room at a time. We compiled an action plan using the 10 principles listed in this book and she was instructed to carry them out over at least a 12- week period. She took it one step at a time and when the whole house was redecorated, she moved into the family home with a positive feeling.

Some time after that, she came to see me again. She was beginning to hear people talk to her that belonged to others around her. She was ecstatic at this. I looked at her again and noticed she was practically glowing. Yes, she was still sad, but she was ready.

'Jennifer, your vibrational level is now at a point where it can see and hear spirit. You are glowing and I am so proud of you. You are also ready to meet someone else. You do feel this happening don't you?'

'Yes, I do as a matter of fact. Actually, I met a guy on Saturday night. His name is Mark and he is absolutely gorgeous!'

(Was this the same girl that was adamant that she would never ever be with someone again?)

You know, we are two years on and she has settled a lot. No more panic attacks and depression. She has settled back into the family home and she has a new love. She has experienced a great loss yet had the courage to reach out to help that was offered. We are all self-healing. Time is good but we need other tools as well. We need to use what god gave us and that is the energy within us all.

As a medium, I say to people when they ask if spirit really do exist. The saying goes, 'seeing is believing' but I like to say, 'believing is seeing'. That belief is faith and faith is something that you don't have to go to church to have, it is within us all.

Jennifer says that Cal gave her faith to go on. What I saw was Jennifer having faith that Cal was right there with her. That faith was due to the evidence that he produced that Mothering Sunday. Faith is all knowing and no seeing. Once established within, it's pretty unshakeable and takes root and transfers to other things. We develop an inner strength and courage, two symptons of Faith. Jennifer also went onto raise money for charity and has started her own business in hairdressing to provide for her children. she has begun to 'read' for other people and considers her hearing spirit as something quite spectacular declaring that if everyone knew how simple it was to be connected and if they but only knew how marvellous they would feel when they are 'plugged in' they would realise how they had only be living a half life beforehand. I liked the way she put that!

## But what is FAITH?

Faith is something that has often gone un-quantified. Much is made of faith being something that is branded about at churches and only happens to people that have a belief system in God (Universal energy, Source, Divine Spirit, Heavenly Father etc) which is not really correct. As a medium, the common perception of us is that we are terrible people who descend from the 'dark side' or the 'Devil' himself and are deluded or mentally ill!! Then how come most of us believe in God and the existence of a higher power? Of course we do! If we believe in the survival of the spirit after the physical death then we believe in the holy-spirit. But how do we really know that the big man exists? We don't, not *really* but we have faith that he does. When you understand that everything has energy and nothing ever just ceases to exist then you begin to wonder that just maybe there has to be something else. Our 'subconscious' mind processes all that we don't see. Used correctly, and with positive intent, we harness our belief system along with the power of the subconscious mind and our thoughts to produce '**faith**'. You see, we all want to believe but we let society cloud our judgement. If you are the type of person that allows yourself to do what others say you should do and you know that you will do damage to yourself, would you partake in doing it? Exactly! All around us we have advertisers saying eat this and eat that, drink this and drink that and couple that with experiences they catch you at a week moment and you say, 'Oh go on then, once won't hurt' and pretty soon you make excuses as to why you need to still eat what you eat and drink what you drink. When our faith becomes damaged it is very easy to go along a path that leads to you destructing your own body. We are quick to persecute drug addicts but do you honestly think that they got up one day and said 'I know, lets take drugs and continue taking them until I am no longer here or do serious damage to myself' Of course not! Yet, that is what you are doing to YOU. We use food to feed our emotions like drug addicts or alcoholics do to drown or surpress their emotions in basically the same way yet we often act self-righteous towards these poor people thinking that we are ok, we have nothing going on in our background. Faith therefore is something that we have that becomes damaged due to circumstance, experience and negative thinking. Yet faith does 'drive' us. Without it, it is impossible to lose the weight and keep it off. It's an important part of who we are and we all have to have **Faith** in something, whether it is God, us, life, somebody we love. Faith inspires us, guides us, motivates us, can help to keep us in line and makes us ask questions. By having that faith in who we are can bring about a change in our whole spiritual being and our bodies will respond accordingly to maintain a healthy weight. But it needs help. The body therefore reflects the mind and spirit. Each one has a profound effect on the other and so on and so forth. So lets get cracking with the faith, which will improve our whole spirit and then the body and we can be all we can be and more.

**On a religious note..**
God gave us churches as havens, places to go to, to be safe and to pray and be closer to him. Then came the good book, the 'Bible' still the most sold book in the world today. This book surely was designed to keep us on the straight and narrow, to give us insight and strength and courage when needed. Not to be used as a crutch. I think the 'big guy' knew what he was talking about. The praying in itself will make us feel good. Recent studies have shown that when a group of people pray for the health of an individual to get better (without that individual knowing) the healing rate is accelerated compared to the individuals who have had no praying done for them. Praying on a personal level is in itself a fabulous thing. It raises our individual vibrational level. Confessing will help us to discard our baggage and lighten our load that we carry (a problem shared is a problem halved after all) singing will make our heart

soar and once again, our vibrational level will raise. Sending healing thoughts and thoughts of helping others, again, will raise the vibrational level. Then the punch line, 'Ask and ye shall receive!'

Yes, the 'big guy' knew what he was talking about and we are only getting it now . . .

*'When you are inspired by some great purpose, some extraordinary project, all your thoughts will break their bonds: Your mind transcends limitations, your consciousness expands in every direction, and you find yourself in a new, great, and wonderful world. Dormant forces, faculties and talents become alive, and you discover yourself to be a greater person by far than you ever dreamed yourself to be.'*
(Patanjali, the ancient Indian philosopher and Yogi)

Let's be clear about one thing. Each of you is a remarkable human being capable of doing so much. I am constantly astounded at the strength of the human spirit, the emphasis being on the word spirit. If you have ever seen someone who has died, you will look at them and just 'know' that it is not 'them'. The very essence of them no longer is there, it has left the body. The spirit makes you who you are. It is our physical self that gives us limitations. We often weigh this down by being heavy adding to our limitations.

When something happens that excites you, isn't it a marvellous feeling? How would you like to feel like that constantly? You would love to wouldn't you!

First things first, get a project. Having a purpose gives your life more meaning. We all have to have a dream, a goal or a vision. It's what we aspire to and how we go about it, defines us. Living means being alive and making the most of it.

Alan, a client of mine was a broken man when I initially saw him. His partner had gone back to her ex and he was devastated. Now, Alan was a very down to earth man with traditional values. His mother and father were still together and his sister was in a long-term marriage and his brother was too. Due to depression, he had got himself into a very negative thinking pattern, bad debt and was on the verge of losing his home, car and was drinking to excess. Alan had lost the love of his life to her ex-husband and felt lied to and cheated on. Understandably, he struggled. But through the dark forest he was in, he somehow found his way to seek help so I knew that a bigger part of him wanted to get to a place that was debt free, happy and in a good place so that he could somehow fall in love again.

Now, men do 'work' differently to women. They are wired up differently (as a friend of mine who is also male can't help but tell me every time I see him!) but I believe that the ten step action plan and over 12 weeks will work for men just as well if not better (their black and white perspective means they decide and just get on with it unlike us women who deliberate for a while first)

I looked into his eyes as I 'read' for him first and then we drew up his individual plan for him to work in with his life. I have to say, Alan totally handed himself over to me in a bid to feel better and that most definitely helped!

We arranged to meet after the 12 weeks with weekly phone calls for support.

I have included Alan's case after the quote from the Indian Yogi because he stood out so much in my mind that I felt I had to honour him as being someone who displayed such unfailing faith that it still to this day inspires me to refer to how strong his constitution was and still is.

Alan is a Drystane Dyker to trade. He admits himself he is not academically bright but what he lacks in that department he more than makes up from with his graft. Slowly and surely over a few months, he stuck to his plan religiously. He moved back home to save money. He borrowed a sum of money from his sister and set up a consultancy business alongside his subcontracting business to make money in a different area and broaden his earning capacity. He got rid of his expensive car, sold his motorbike (this was a biggie for Alan) and got down to some hard graft. The female looked for a while like she was trying to keep him sweet just in case the relationship with her ex-husband (she has three children with him and he used to hit her too) didn't work out. Alan swayed momentarily with this but I reminded him of his plan, and he stuck to it. He was comfort eating also when I initially saw him but as the weeks progressed, Alan felt more in control. His mother took charge and cooked healthy meat and three vegetable meals. He started to come to my classes too and got himself different friends that had a broad spectrum of interests. Alan began to laugh again.

Our contact dwindled when Alan felt more in charge of his life. He started another relationship with a woman but it fell through after a few months when she got too clingy. Alan, continued to work really hard and now has over a years supply of work that takes him abroad as well. He came to see me recently proudly declaring that he had finally paid off all the money he owed his sister, his next target being to save for a new and more reliable car and his plans to expand abroad were taking shape. He had met a lovely girl who works in a solicitors office and is taking things slowly but he is quietly optimistic and has is happy and content. Success!! It means different things to different people. Alan learned to transcend his mind past all his limitations as he focused on his goals and aspirations. He discovered that there was more to him than he thought previously. His heart soared as he successfully forged his way through the haze of grief and disappointment. He learned to laugh again and this raised his vibartional level to one where he experienced such force that he acknowledged something greater than him.

Yes, I am proud of Alan for he has shown what a person can do and how inspired action can completely turn your life around!

# CHAPTER FIVE

# Funny old life-ain't it?

*HOW DO WE EVER HAVE THE FAITH TO CARRY ON IN THE FACE OF ADVERSITY IF SOMEONE FIRST DIDN'T SHOW THAT FAITH IN US? BE THE FAITH YOU WANT TO SEE.*
*(LARA WELLS)*

Through the years I have discovered that not controlling the emotional response to circumstance is rather like a racehorse running loose. Now if a racehorse is running loose we would have to find some way of catching it and controlling it wouldn't we? Of course we would. It's a safety thing! Racehorses can be nervous animals and often possess nervous energy that when handled properly can be fantastic. Handled improperly and without the right raining plan and confidence training it could go horribly wrong-a disaster when there is often so much money involved never mind the mental welfare of the animal.

I used to work with racehorses when I first left school at the tender age of 16. I saw some sights and spent most of my time either rehabilitating the mess that others created or schooling the babies (a very important job you will understand as it could either make or break the horse)

We would buy horses from a country where they would break their horses in 3 days. Bridle on the horse and being led on the 1st day, saddle and girth on the 2nd day and rider on and down the track on the 3rd day-scary or what! Can you even begin to imagine the psychological damage done to the horse never mind it's temperament by the time another yard had bought the horse?

I once had a horse under my wing that had half an ear, scars all down the its chest and legs, and a back like 'the Malvern Hills' This horse couldn't even walk straight let along go on a racecourse. It kept dumping the jockeys and bombing out of the race in the wrong direction and soon earned itself a reputation in the 'race-form' book as 'Not to be trusted…and very unlikely that this horse will ever see a racecourse again' The owner transferred this horse to our yard after all jockeys refused to ride this particular horse and for a while he just stood in the corner of his new abode with his bottom lip down and his head down. Now stick with me because there is a good reason I am telling you this story. I know not all of you are horsy people but we learn by life. Animals or people, we have spirit and energy so aren't we the same really?

I was assigned this horse and to begin with he wouldn't even take a carrot from my outstretched hand. I remember standing at his door, looking in night after night, morning after morning, day after day and not once did I ever even see him eat his food placed for him in his basin. Nobody else would have anything to do with him and yet there was something about him. I thought to myself that if I had had a rough time and everyone gave up on me, how would I feel? Surely we all deserve somebody to be there and should we ever stop trying?

So, I began my 'therapy' and entered his stable a few times a day. Every half hour I went to see him. I made sure I spoke constantly to him and patted him and stroked him. To begin with he would shy away and turn his back on me and would 'hide' in the corner. He would turn his head to me and put his one and a half ears flat back against his head and show me his teeth to try and scare me away. But I persevered. I felt his back and he flinched and tried to bite me so I figured that the main problem was his back. This horse was in agony. How would I feel if I had a bad back and somebody was asking me to jump massive fences never mind ride me? So, I organised for the 'back man' to come to see him every 3 days and every day twice a day I put the blanket on that contained magnets and electrical currents rather like a bigger version of the 'tens Machine' that people use for pain relief. This stimulates the body to produce its own natural pain relief. He still wouldn't speak to me or face me when I spoke to him-in fact he said nothing at all.

One day I had an accident when I was riding out and was later back from morning exercise. As I approached limping to the yard holding the reins of the horse I was leading, I heard a banging noise and very, very loud screaming. My man was going absolutely frantic in his box. Then he saw me and stopped briefly before whinnying with absolute delight. He spoke! He had noticed I was late and became worried. I ran over to him after putting my charge in its box and cuddled him where we held each other for what seemed like ages and from that point onwards he watched for me coming every morning and every half hour after that. The tables had turned, he was now looking out for me.

A few weeks after later, he allowed me to mount him and ride him gently and we worked over the next few weeks to get his confidence back up and I spoke to him constantly, reassuring him all the time of how well he was doing and would inform him beforehand of what we were going to do.

Eventually, the owner asked if we could ever get him on the racecourse again and I pondered. The owners were eternally grateful that we had their 'boy' back but I was not sure about putting back on a track again with someone who didn't' know or understand him. All he wanted was to be understood and to be treated fairly. I thought and I thought. I spoke it over with him and conferred with the 'back man' and I researched his last races and then it hit me-all his races had been on right handed tracks (The track bended to the right) When he jumped before, his back had been so bad, he kept jumping to the left often going into other horses and riders or jumping away from the race. He had been in pain and was trying to protect his rider when he 'dumped' them not out of being nasty!! Of course, if we put him on a left handed track, he would be jumping in the race and would be happier (You have to understand that they even put blinkers on him thinking that the other horses were putting him off or they used them thinking he was 'dishonest'!!) It was his back that gave him his main problem and now we had built up his confidence, we could work on that and see if he could do it. My boy was fast and a stayer and he loved to race-when he is happy.

So, we tentatively entered him in a £40,000 race. This was a lot of money 20 years ago and was a good sign of the class of runners he was with and how capable he was. Well, you should've seen what was written about him in the papers. The 'experts' were absolutely laughing their heads off that 'my boy' had even set foot on a racecourse again let alone in such a class of race. We had enlisted a good jockey with lovely sensitive hands who had ridden him at home and they got on really well. He took some stick as well. It was a fabulous sight to see 'my boy' walking calmly to the starting line. Out of eight fantastic horses with impeccable form, 'my boy' finished third!! We couldn't believe it. I can't tell you how proud I was of him. And you should've seen his face. He calmly walked into the ring in third place like he knew he could do it. I hugged him with sheer delight at what he had accomplished.

The owners entered him into another race. This time there were 12 runners. We kept up the back therapy and the papers said this time, instead of mocking him, that he was the 'dark horse' of the pack and watch him with interest. The race was another £40,000 race and a left- handed track with no blinkers. This time, he strode onto the track, me talking to him all the time, stroking his neck and telling him how fantastic he was. I let him got. This time, ladies and gentlemen, this time he won!

The power and strength of someone having faith in you, the contact and someone just 'being there' the sending the message that they could rely on me, and the team of people we had built around him. Yes, he was a horse. Would he have known the words I was using or the tone and reassurance of my voice? The motivation tone telling him he could do it when all the odds and majority or people were stacked against him? He didn't know that. He only knew how he felt as how he felt made a drastic difference to his mental state of mind that then affected his physical body. I worked on his mind and got the specialists to give him natural pain relief for his back and pretty soon he felt better in himself and the his confidence soared and his mind healed his body. He felt great and his body took shape to mirror his mind. That horse that everybody had written off won his race and against some of the best racehorses in his time. Proving to me beyond all doubt that how you think affects how you feel and how you feel affects the body. Therefore, by slimming your life you can indeed slim your body, ridding it of all the emotional baggage and scars that we don't see to eat healthy because we feel healthy and then we look healthy.

Are each of us any different to that horse? Can we make our bodies into a fuel- efficient machine that when well oiled and treated with respect, we can get the best from it? Of course we can.

Remember:

No one can make you feel inferior without your permission (Eleanor Roosevelt)

CHAPTER 6

# YOU ARE WHAT YOU EAT/YOU EAT WHAT YOU ARE

*Habit is habit and not to be flung out of the window by any man, but coaxed downstairs a step at a time.*
(Mark Twain)

Most of us eat as to how we feel. We are trained at a very early age that we have time we have to eat and our body clock is set to that. We are trained to eat because it is lunch-time and not because we are hungry. This is due to conditioning at a very early age. Babies were in my day fed every 4 hours. Now it doesn't take Einstein to work out that that would be a breakfast time 8 am, lunch- time of 12 pm, tea-time of 4 pm and then supper-time of 8 pm. Now the times may vary with you all reading this but you get the picture. Then we grow a bit and are then weaned with snacks as well. At no point did anybody train me out of that. Even my Nan always had food around every 2 hours to accommodate main meals and snacks. Now anyone that knew my Nan would confirm that she was always the first one in at the buffet and the last one to leave. Hmmm. I also grew up with her proudly declaring that I was 'from her side of the family'. So, don't really need to understand that genetic factors and conditioning have a lot to do with my own personal battle against the bulge then! However, it did occur to me that my Nan hid a lot and used food to compensate for something that was missing. The only place she was ever really happy was when she was down south, Buckingham to be exact. My Nan did not like being so far away from her birthplace and family and now I understand that she had resorted to 'feed' her child within as it prompted good memories of being 'home'. She was unhappy and my grandfather, due to all the travel he did in his working life, refused on retiring, to go and life back down south. He was a good man and she had been brought up to respect her husband's wishes so she stayed here, against hers. By feeding her and her family (constantly) she satisfied her longing to go home.

Now, I am not suggesting that you all whip the suitcases out from under the bed and start packing by any stretch of the imagination. What I am trying to do, however, is to understand about conditioning and family traits. Often, how you eat is not your fault but once you realise that this has contributed you realising that you have a problem, then it is your responsibility to re-educate those negative feeding patterns out and this should be done gradually but firmly. The other matter is of course how long does one have to do a routine before it becomes a habit? Astronauts are best placed to answer this question. They go through extremely rigorous training indeed but the one problem they encountered was that once they are out of our gravitational field, there is nothing to 'hold' them there and they would turn around and perform their tasks not to mention everything else, upside down! We are used to the opposite. So they designed apparatus that when worn would make them see everything upside down in preparation for their mission. It was difficult at first but none of them wanted to admit defeat and stuck it out. Then something amazing happened. After 12 weeks, the eyes started to see without the eye- wear everything upside down! The brain had gathered enough evidence for it to learn and re-wire itself to convert the images it saw and place them upside down so the astronauts didn't have to wear the goggles-amazing! We are amazing it seems and this experiment has enabled us to now understand a bit more of how the brain works. 12 weeks is all the brain needs to compile enough information to make the changes you are instilling, a bit like uploading information and allowing time for it to compute and activate those changes into action.

Changing your eating habits will therefore work in the same principle which is a bit different to what the slimming classes will tell you. The average length of time that an average member stays in the one class is 8 weeks. That's why prepaid vouchers are in 4 weeks and 8 week bundles. We are taught that we need 6 weeks to change bad habits and 6 weeks for new habits to take their place, which is true making it the 12 weeks that the astronaut experiment told us. The average member often doesn't make it to the 12 week mark, however, giving up before then thinking they can do it all on their own.

Like my four legged horse friend, he thrived when I unconditionally gave him the help he needed. He responded in the best way he could, by proving them all wrong and winning his race after his mind and health improved.

**Then why do we think that we can do it on our own?**

If you look at any successful person around you or in the media, (go on-google it if you must) then you will see that they are successful due to the people they surround themselves with. They have a team of professionals, friends and family who support them and who all have their talents that when used together, work really well.

Then ask that same question again- Why **do** you think you can do this on your own?

Support is a great thing to have. That's why I have written this book. To support and encourage you and to help you understand that the only person holding you back is - **YOU!**

Now, this book is not just for weight loss. It is a book that will get you to dump that unnecessary baggage from your mind that is holding you back from your body achieving its natural healthy weight. If it is not healthy, then it shows on your body. Realise this and also the saying 'Seeing is believing' and begin to see that you are the master of your own destiny. When you can 'see' that you are more than capable of having a mental 'clear-out' like you would clear out your bedroom or sitting room, then you can believe that the ideal body is yours for the taking.

One of my clients was going though a particularly tricky time. Her husband had just left her for another woman, she was 5 months pregnant, 3 other children, had £4 in her purse, and she then discovered that she was getting evicted from the house due to him not paying the rent. (There was 6 months unpaid rent and she had given him the money each month to pay it but he clearly hadn't used it for the rent leaving her in dire straits)

You can see even by the information so far that she was in a pretty desperate place. A survivor of breast cancer in her mid twenties, (her mother died from the third appearance of it a few years later) my client, Lynda, had also had to terminate a little boy so that she could have the treatment her breast cancer needed to be banished.

Lynda was stunned that she had been through so much before and the marriage had survived and now she had to cope with all that she was left with.

Initially Lynda came to see me for me to hopefully tell her that her estranged husband was coming back to her. I couldn't tell her what I didn't feel was true. Deep down she knew this to be true too.

So, we set about building her life plan up and to do that we had to look at why she allowed her life to spiral out of control. Lynda had to confront some home truths some of which are as follow:

She changed what she wanted to what her husband wanted and had forgotten her own goals and aspirations.

Had handed over all income and all control to her husband so her choices became extremely limited.

Gave him too much freedom

Tried to 'fix' him.

And these were just a few of them.

Lynda is a gorgeous, extremely articulate woman with a fantastic personality. Due to the problems that had developed over the years prior to the break up, she gained a huge amount of weight. The problem, the stress and issues of married life had 'blocked' her and sent her energy out of balance and it had pulled her vibrational level down until it felt like a lead weight. Her weight through all this ballooned until she had something else to be unhappy about other than her failing marriage.

Lynda had acknowledged that in order to ignore what was really causing her stress, her body had created another one for her to switch her unhappiness too. Her husband even had the audacity to blame her being overweight as a factor for him to leave her when in fact the unhappiness and repression had caused this and he was actually the cause.

Lynda, being a diet fanatic in the past, had written a weekly planner and daily diary on what she had eaten for the six months prior to her seeing me. It was clear that the quantity of what she was eating was not the problem. Rather, it was that she wasn't eating enough and then substituting with the wrong foods to suppress the low moods and give them the reward of a short-lived boost to get a 'high' of energy temporarily.

We discussed many aspects of her life and we came up wit a plan. This was to use positive action and take charge of her own life so that she felt in control. I made suggestions but I allowed her to make the decision ultimately, reinforcing any suggestions she made and being an inner voice:

Her list for the 'New Her' went as follows:

1.  Sort her finances/get a job/do a course
2.  Move house into town so less on travel
3.  Walk everywhere
4.  Plan on what to eat daily-stick to it
5.  Go out with friends twice a month
6.  Change her hair
7.  Body piercing/tattoos
8.  Establish a new friendship circle
9.  Sort out any legal issues
10. Get custody and visitation rites organised.
11. Get her breast re-construction and tummy tuck

Lynda made this the plan that she wanted with the overall view that she was going to change her life. She got back in control. Did what she said she was going to do mainly because she was letting herself down more than anything and there was no excuse for that now. To date, Lynda has lost five and a half stone, has had her tummy tuck and the first part of her reconstruction, a prolapse operation, has moved into town, got a new job, several body piercings and a tattoo, new friends, got purple lowlights, and has control of her finances with plans for a business venture and designs or a new man! Lynda is a reformed character who is just such a different girl from the one I saw a couple of years ago. Her daughter is now 2 years old and is a very welcome addition to her family. Lynda is about to become a grandmother as I write this and I am privileged to have been part of her life as she has made those changes.

We are brought up to resist change yet when action is applied, it can be a positive thing. We regard it as going against what we are used to and it unearths all that we are familiar with. As people, we should embrace change. Lynda just needed the help to make those changes in the absence of the person in her life that would normally help her make them.

So, to help you on your way, what do you say? We need a plan, oh yes we doodi...

*There is nothing permanent except change.*
(Heraclitus)

# CHAPTER 7

# LET'S MAKE A PLAN THAT WILL PLAN TO MAKE US

*IF YOU FAIL TO PLAN,*
*THEN YOU ARE PLANNING TO FAIL*
(Anonymous)

Planning is something that has taken me many years to do. My parents didn't instil it in me preferring to let life unfold on its own. My brother drifted into a life that remains to this day, one of drug use and unfortunately mental health problems caused by them. I am sure he didn't 'plan' to do that, he just drifted into that kind of lifestyle brought on by the embracing of the 'rave' culture in the nineties. Sad as it is, one can't help but wonder that if he had some kind of a game plan and goal, he would've been more likely to have got himself back on track.

Now, I find these issues hard to talk about. I love my brother but have looked after him for the last 20 years. Those years have been extremely hard work (part of my psychological baggage) and contributed to many a heated disagreement at home. I have many clients that have lost their children through drugs and consider myself lucky that it could be much worse. Life doesn't always turn out how you expect. You are probably reading this right now and mentally going through a few issues of your own. Good, for it is important to know, that even when you feel that life is at it's darkest, we all have them.

Children are something that we tend to take for granted. I have clients that have been trying for children and really struggle hitting home that if you can have children naturally, then you are very lucky indeed!

Recently, a client came to see me and we addressed the issue of children and she whipped out a sheet of paper (well a few actually) and proceeded to show me her graphs, her plan of action, her vitamin intake and her healthy diet. Wow! Now this was impressive. I had told her at our last session that if she were to bake a cake, would she not use the finest ingredients to bake this cake so that she could be sure that she was doing everything possible for the best cake to be baked and by doing everything she could that when the cake were in the oven, she could be sure that it would rise to be magnificent and a testament to her hard work she had put it beforehand? Of course she would. So, she had gone away and made a plan, and boy, had she made a plan!

Three months later and guess what? You said it, pregnant! Delighted as she was, she said that making the plan and following it had taken her mind of the trying and hey presto, a little girl followed that December.

If you speak to any successful person, you will be told that all of them start out with a plan in mind to take them to a particular goal. If there is not plan involved, then they have no guidelines and they will get sidetracked or lose the momentum. Even when going to the bank to ask for a loan, they like to see a business plan, don't they?

Now take a moment to think when the last time it was that you made a plan and followed it to get to a particular goal. Do you have a goal?

Assuming that you are reading this book to lose weight (although you can use the template for more than that) would you say that you usually start slimming with great gusto and fall by the wayside after a while? Why would you say this was?

Goals are extremely important for every aspect of your life. Even from a place of attracting things to you (we will cover this in the next chapter) you have to send out a message for something specific and if you waver from this it's like sending out mixed messages-which one is it you want?

I have asked over a thousand people before writing this book if they had a goal in life and the people that didn't have a goal admitted in my survey that they were a bit 'lost' and when pressed for the reason why, they said that they had been brought up with no expectations so had not really had any themselves.

Your perception of yourself and the perception that others have of you are two different things entirely. For example, people may see you as strong and confident, yet you feel shy and inhibited. So at some point, you have made the conscious decision to allow people to think that and put on a good performance (so to speak) therefore you have made a decision somewhere haven't you?

When you get up in the morning you decide to put your clothes on. Is it because you have been taught to do that as you have been conditioned to or is it because you have decided that if you don't, you will be naked and others will stare? This is probably a silly example but the whole point being that your life is full of decision making. Whether they are everyday decisions or massive life changing decisions, you make them.

Then why is it that we often stay in a situation when we know or feel that it is so wrong for us and is making us unhappy? Change can be a frightening thing but surely the prospect of staying in a bad relationship or in a situation that is not right for us is even more frightening than doing something about it? Why if we are capable of making small decisions are we then deemed incapable of making larger ones?

1. Right now I want you to decide on a few things. Are you?
2. In a good relationship
3. Where you want to be in your career/Job

4.   Happy with the effort you are making
5.   Happily married/living together
6.   Healthy
7.   Fit
8.   A friend to someone or many
9.   In a good place financially
10.  Able to progress with your dreams
11.  Happy

The last one is very necessary. Happiness means different things to different people but I mean 'happy' as you would describe happy. You would know if you were 'happy' as it is an emotional connection and contentedness that surpasses all other emotions. You reach state that is what I would call as 'bliss'. My cousin has a saying 'Don't bug my happiness' which is very apt at times!

In order to feel happy you first have to 'know' that you are happy and I will tell you how to do that in the next chapter.

For now **you** need **you** to make a plan. On it you are going to make a list of goals on the top of the page. You may have a plan in a few areas. For example, with work, you may have a goal, with your figure, you may have a size you want to get into, with your finances, you may want to start and save an amount each month for 'just in case' with the end result being enough for a deposit for a flat or property. Either way, if one goal is not enough for you broaden it out a bit.

Every morning, noon and night, you can get this plan out and have a look to re-affirm your goals. When you are looking in the mirror, say them to yourself 9 times. Smile as well as this will promote a happy feeling. When you are on the phone can you tell if the other person is smiling as they are talking? I can. When they are not smiling, they sound depressed and boring, when they smile, it lifts the voice and you 'feel' the other person smiling so you automatically think they are happy. Try, walking down the street and smiling spontaneously at the person coming towards you. Do this a few times. Some will automatically smile at you, some will forget themselves momentarily then revert back to looking sad. Some will carry on smiling. Result!

If you say those goals with a smile on your face, this lifts the voice and as you hear the voice in its lifted tones you will feel happy because you hear a happy tone. This will have an effect on you over time and before you know it, you feel more positive all round. Fantastic job you are doing there!

Now, I am aware that we discussed eating the right foods for lifting the vibrations and chapter 10 will show you these foods and recipes. With this planning sheet-photo copy another 3 sheets because we are going to do a rotational 4 weeks so that your metabolism won't slow with it thinking that you are eating less in the way of calories and are making every effort to keep it interested. I like to think of the metabolism as a separate person. If you treat it in this way, you begin to understand it a bit better. The higher the vibrational level - the higher the metabolism. What these foods do along with dumping the mind baggage is it will 'free' the vibration it is working on to work in with your body's natural frequency. Then with using this plan, it will raise it further to promote a magnificent sense of well -being, good health and good fortune. As I said to someone recently when they said that being slim would make them happy, I then replied,

'first you must be happy then your body will be slim.'

*"Well," said Pooh, "what I like best," and then he had to stop and think. Because although eating honey was a very good thing to do, there was a moment just before you began to eat it which was better than when you were, but he didn't know what it was called.*

(A.A. Milne)

The thought of eating something you shouldn't is a bit like eating somebody else's chips, fabulous! But when you buy your own, they never taste the same. Therefore, if you were to plan ahead and be organised, you would have everything to hand. Whatever you think you want is never the same as when you give in to temptation. Now you know why it is great to have a plan. The happy bit happens just before you eat it and now whilst you are, remember that!

*'We all cling to the past,*
*and because we cling to the past,*
*we become unavailable*
*to the present'*
(Author Unknown)

# CHAPTER 8

# AS YOU ARE AND SO IT IS

*Work, like you don't need money,*
*Love, like you've never been hurt,*
*And dance, like no one's watching.*
(An old Irish Proverb)

I have lost count of how many times I have been approached by someone with the immortal words 'I wish I could see and hear spirit' Although this is a book about slimming your life to lose weight in all areas and not just physically, it will have the added benefit of helping those of you who are hoping to master the skills you possess to be a medium or a healer. We all have the ability to do this, it's just more pronounced in some than others. You are encouraged to draw at school and we all can, but have you noticed that some are exceptional at it and some are only just ok? Of course you have. Musicians are the same, authors and poets too. We each have a gift and the fine-tuning will begin from what you already have.

By planning, using the techniques in this book and eating the right foods, you can help you life the most enlightened life, feel uplifted, positive and happy and guess what? This will show in all other areas too. The quotation at the beginning of this chapter is my favourite one, the end sentence of the proverb has absolute clarity for me, 'Dance like no one's watching' how true is that! In other words, you get on with doing what you have to do and forget all the negative things that have happened up to the point you have decided to do something about it. Have a goal and go for it and be undeterred by what could possibly hold you back. Live life as you mean it and not just half- heartedly.

The reason I asked ask people the questions in my phase assessment is to give me an idea of what they have had to go through to become who they are today. The idea after that is for YOU to self recognise and acknowledge how far you have come. Then we draw a line under it and that's when your goals come into it. Before you set the goals, it will be an idea to meditate and allow yourself to come to terms with the past. I have designed some specific meditations for this that you can purchase and I have a dear friend, Mark Brandist, who does fabulous meditations for enlightenment and his meditations are excellent too. I would fully recommend that you do these meditations for at least 12 weeks. Think of them as a prescription, rather like your own doctor would prescribe (like antibiotics) wouldn't you take them for a designated time as advised? Then give my recommendation the same courtesy and do the same, I may not be a doctor, but I know how to increase my vibrational level to speak to spirit and along the way, discovered how to use that same vibrational level to 'attract' what I want in life. For a while I assumed that what I needed was enough. But then I distinguished the difference between what I need and what I want and threw off my limiting beliefs that stopped me from asking. I began to realise that in order to help others, I had to ask for more - and ask I did! Nothing prepared me for the response. I received all right!

Now, like many of you reading Spiritual Slimming, you have probably read multiple books on the Law of Attraction, The globally recognised book The Secret, Esther and Gerry Hick's wonderful books with Abraham channelling, Joe Vitale's The Missing Secret, Byron Katie's A Thousand Names for Joy and Louse L Hay's amazing books to name but a few. Yet, fantastically inspiring as they were, me being me wondered in a practical way, how your average every day person could incorporate that into their life and carry it off successfully. I asked, and then I received in the most unexpected of ways.

When Luke (my fourth son) and his sister, Tabitha go to country dancing practice after school, I usually take my third son, Nathanael, out for a drink and a chat, take him shopping for books and generally have some quality mother and son time when it is just him and I.

Anyway, there we were just leaving the place we were chatting in and having a drink (well ok, it was a Christian Bookshop) and a phone call later, we were instructed to go to another shop for some frozen vegetables. I met someone who had been in the audience of an event I had taken part in very recently and we got to talking. The conversation was very funny and I had her laughing her socks off. As we had no car with us as it was being valletted, we decided to get a taxi but it was tea time and the busy time of the day when we were extremely unlikely to get one. Still laughing I said to my son as we walked away form the shop,

'Wouldn't it be fabulous if a taxi just came around the corner right now?' and he said

'Mum, it's tea time, the chance would be a fine thing-oh look, there's a flying pig!' (a saying we all say when there is no chance!)

We laughed some more and as I looked up, no word of a lie, a taxi appeared out of nowhere and was crawling around the corner of the road in front of us. It slowed even more and I lowered myself to see the driver. He slowly rolled the window down and I asked him if he was on a fare and he said no. So I put my hand out and sprinted across the road before anybody else appeared, bags flying all over the place. I was stunned!

Clambering in the front seat of the car I asked him if he usually crawled along roads like that (he honestly appeared from nowhere) to which he replied,

'I had a sudden urge to drive around that corner slowly as I just knew somebody was needing me there and no-I don't usually kerb crawl!' oops, sometimes my wording can sound a bit iffy but he knew what I meant. I looked back at my son and he looked at me. I then had a 'WOW' moment as I realised that that was how you asked for things. Simply asking for the sake of it doesn't work. But ask, sound happy and feel happy and you get-unconditionally!

So, how you feel is down to how you think. Think happy and you will feel happy and when you feel happy, ask for what you want. Don't be afraid to as this adds purpose. I used to be afraid, as I had been brought up with manners that made me put others before myself. I would always wait at the end of the queue for what was left, always make sure that others had a choice and I was left with no choice at all and always would be the one the eventually no one would give any weight to. My opinions no longer counted, I felt that I was no longer worthy and I got depressed. I STILL put other first until one day I wondered why we didn't get invited to parties and functions. People were happy to take from me without giving back because I felt embarrassed to ask for anything in return thinking that I would get respect for it. In short, people walked all over me!

Now, I ask so that I can give to them and instead of taking the very essence of me, I have something in reserve for them and they get a bit of both. After all, I'm not much good if I make myself ill whilst helping others, am I?

I think a lot of my thoughts on this came from the realisation that, a lot of people in this industry have major health problems. I had to ask myself why this was mainly because I had five children to be here for and as the main breadwinner, I couldn't afford to be ill. Was it possible that they the doing the same and not noticing that they were giving themselves away and asking nothing back. I don't mean money as I absolutely think that it is perfectly acceptable to ask for compensation for your time and gift that is invaluable to another. It's an energy thing. What do you replace that with?

How do you feel when you read this? Do you think you are allowing the same thing to happen to you? Do you feel invisible, not by choice but by accident?

The main frame (this is a term I use for the Spiritual Matrix) is something that works on a give and take basis. I thought that if you give first, then you will get back. What happens if it is not until 15 years down the line and in the meantime, your life as gone to the wall?

The bible is still the most highly sold book in the world. Nobody has ever seen god, but millions and millions pray to him every day of every, week. He has different names too but he is the one and the same. God is a vast and magnificent 'energy' and he exists in the mainframe along with the spirits of your loved one, your guides, guardians, gatekeepers and angels. We don't all believe in his existence but lets face it, unless you have had to ask those questions in life, do we every really need to explore the whole principle and experience of such an existence? No, probably not. Some people just 'know' he exists and some spend their entire life carrying out experiments and looking for the 'proof'. Like I said in a previous chapter, they like to think that they will believe it when they see it when it is in fact 'believe and you will see'.

This whole energy exchange works on the same principle. It helps if you believe that it will happen then it will. You shouldn't first wait and see what happens then you will believe that it works!

Love is the highest vibration known. Love is something that can happen without you knowing about it and trust me when I say, you don't choose who you fall in love with, it just happens. Somewhere deep inside of us we have a kind of radar, an energy if you like, that seeks. It is programmed to do so without your knowledge and acts of its own accord. This is the same radar that can tell you spirit are there even if you can't physically see them, the same radar that can tell if someone is lying to you, the same radar that just knows when someone loves you even if they say differently. This radar is capable of finding a match all on its own and it will do if you allow it to. That explains why you can absolutely think that someone is gorgeous but your friends look at you like you are really weird because they think he is really ugly!

So, if your energy is capable of doing all that, falling in love, seeing spirit, telling if someone is lying, even finding your way to a destination without having the directions if you let it work properly that is (I once found our way to a campsite in France in the dark after hubby had been driving for 5 hours without success. He had filled the tank with petrol previously, put the directions to the campsite on the roof and promptly drove off without them so being me, I remained patient for the whole 5 hours, then demanded he get out the car, slid into the driving seat and found the site in the dark with no direction in France in 10 minutes!!) That is a built in radar working to its potential and we all have one.

It is said that God created man in the image of himself. Look what god can do and we think we are not able to do the same? Exactly, we 'think' we can't and as the saying goes,

## WHETHER YOU THINK YOU CAN'T OR THINK YOU CAN EITHER WAY YOU ARE PROBABLY RIGHT

Let's use this energy that has been created for us to its best of its ability and be all we can be. Once you realise that each of you has that remarkable power then the world is indeed your oyster and you are that pearl. It can be a job prizing the oyster open but once open you will be free to live your life as you want. You will thrive instead of just survive. I call it being 'plugged into the mainframe' and trust me, when you have experienced the amazing energy from that, you will just *know* the difference.

We all have a value but just because I can do this naturally, it doesn't mean I am more important than you or the next person. However, nobody has the right to make you feel like you have no value without your permission. Take charge of your life and understand that when you do, you will prize open that oyster shell to reveal your pearl.

(Oh and by the way, just thought I'd let you know. Just after I wrote this chapter, my mother called and we spoke about a few things concerning why the ideas she and her partner have had and why they haven't worked. I launched off passionately about my findings and what frame of mind you have to be in before you 'ask' for something. I got to the part about how to view yourself. Kind of like a way of what rewards lie behind all your hard work The oyster and the pearl explanation came into it and I described it like I have just done for you in this chapter. There was a silence from my mother then a giggle. I asked her what she was laughing at and she told me that for my impending birthday (the big 40, I know, hard to believe eh?) She had got a present of a proper pearl and had put it in a box that resembled an oyster shell. I didn't consciously know this, but they say you receive confirmation that you are on the right path at various points in your life. I do believe I have just received mine.

What to do now:

1.   **MEDITATE: (12 weeks then when you need to. Make it a part of your routine)** Do not undervalue the power of the mind. Acknowledge it, use and get it working for you and not against you. As your mind practices to be still, you will find another more powerful part of you that when free, can make such a massive difference I your life. Come on, what are you waiting for, cut it loose!

2.  **DANCE LIKE NO ONE'S WATCHING:** Everyone has a 'type' of music that they like, that inspires them and motivates their energy to feel fantastic. Get it going on people and give it some 'hoofter' Go on, dance like no one's watching and go for it! To live life like you mean it and you don't care whether people judge you or not. We can also say that this means you will become in alignment as it raises the vibration of your individual energy to 'blend' with the god/spirit/cosmic energy that will give/bring you what you ask for.

3.  **MAKE A PLAN AND HAVE A GOAL:** Don't be afraid to ask for what you want and be clear about it or the universal energy will be confused. If you get a mixed message from someone who sends you a text then send you a conflicting text, which one do you take on board and follow up on? Ask for that weight loss, for health, for money, for love, for friends, for a new job. Anything in fact but be clear! Once you have spiritually slimmed and freed up you your vibration, to blend with the energy of the universe, you will have whatever you ask for.

4.  **DON'T WORRY BE HAPPY-SMILE!** As you ask- laugh. Laughter is the best medicine. It releases feel-good endorphins and they give an overall sense of well -being. When you feel that, it generates a sense of happiness and when you ask for what you want, you want the best vibration you can get to go to the organ grinder and not the monkey. Go on, try it! We have all read the books to ask but nobody tells you how to. This is the only book that will, with the right intentions and is spiritually correct. Don't be afraid and feel that you can't ask for money because it's being materialistic, that's just conditioning. We all need to pay bills and keep our overheads going. We need food to eat and children to clothe.

What if you had more? Surely, because you are such giving people and spiritually I just know you would do the right thing, you would use that to help others in the right way? Of course you would. You would be happy because the pressure is off and you would 'glow' vibrationaly because you have the satisfaction of helping others. Let's 'glow' with the flow then. Don't be ashamed. Be encouraged to take inspired action! If people take from you without you having resources to give then they are taking from your very essence. You will become ill after a time and then how many people will you be able to help?

11. **FEED YOUR SOUL:** Eat the right foods to free your vibration to fly where it should fly! Chapter nine is a short chapter but it contains the foods that help your vibration to 'glow' Think of it rather like a huge vibration that has a big elastic band to power it. Overload the elastic belt that drives your machine to give off a vibration and the vibrational level is slow. That overloading is contributed by the foods that we eat. We need food for fuel. If we use the wrong quality of fuel, then wouldn't our engine struggle or not get as much mileage out of it? Of course that would be the case. Most of us *live to eat* when what we really should be doing is *eat to live*. And when we mean live, we mean live well!

How many of you were taught to eat everything on your plate whilst you were growing up? We ignore the signals for stopping with our food levels and we also ignore the signals our body gives us for good quality food that it needs to keep the engine running smoothly. Examine the list I have provided and use these foods in with your daily food intake. Do this gradually until you have weaned yourself off the foods that are holding you back. Because that is what they are doing, holding you back. So stop hiding from what your life can really be like. Dust yourself off and congratulate you for having the courage to be the real you! Well done!

*The things always happen that you really believe in; and the belief in a thing makes it happen.*
(Frank Lloyd Wright)

# CHAPTER NINE

# GOOD, GOOD, GOOD, FOOD VIBRATION

*Without inspiration the best powers of the mind remain dormant.*
*They are a fuel in us, which needs to be ignited with a spark.*
(Johann Gottfried Von Herder)

WATER – a great conductor of electricity and considering your brain is made up of electrical impulses that have to 'fire' a reaction, then, we need water for the conductivity. 7-8 glasses per day. Start off gradually then work your way up. Write a plan of doing this in with your planner and stick to it. You will die far quicker from dehydration than you will of starvation. Shame I know, but without water you can't flush toxins from the blood-stream, or generally aid in the production of healthy cells being produced, renal system working properly and flushing the bugs away. Most people are dehydrated as they don't drink enough.

## Are you getting enough?

Dairy Products. The funny thing is, that cheese, cream, milk and yogurts are a good source of calcium. As a medium, I have to say, that cheese and cream make me ill. I have to listen to my body and understand that if it feels heavy and is struggling in some way, then so are my vibes.

Dairy is cow, cow is a live being and so you must consider that if the milk is making you feel rough, then the cow was probably not happy when milked.

Like with meat, as it is also from a live being, the vibrational content of the meat is dependant on whether the animal was happy or not and lets face it, would you be happy if you knew your life was about to be taken. The stress hormones released into the system form the animal would cause a change to take place and this would be 'remembered' within the meat itself. That said, we do need some of the vitamins from meat so in small moderation, it is appropriate to eat a small amount.

Chicken, turkey and fish is best. Red meat is acceptable but in very small amounts. Stick to meat every second day if you prefer red meat but only 2 ounces at any given meal. I'm sorry if this doesn't agree with some of your principals but I have worked a lot with women and pregnancy and the women who are vegetarians can struggle to fall pregnant and when they introduce a bit of meat into their diet-hey presto, they fall pregnant! The vitamins in raw form from meat are essential. We are carnivores by nature. God provided plants, vegetables and fruit to eat, hens to lay eggs and eat and cattle to eat for the survival of mankind. Being vegetarian, like everything should be in moderation.

It is true that the more spiritually connected you are, the more you taste food, appreciate food and are sensitive to food. Your body will naturally let you know after a while what it needs. Like a child, it is not too clever to give it what it wants all the time but a treat every now and then is acceptable. We aim to live life to the best of our ability but even then, if you let it, the body knows what it wants. If you are in any doubt at all, Kinesiology is a marvellous method to test for what the body 'needs' by using a series of muscle tests. If you are in any doubt at all, try a session or two. You will be amazed at the results.

Again, a lot is down to conditioning. Even slimming clubs have their place and are a marvellous place for support and motivation. This book's aim, like I have said before, is to get you to step into your natural power. To help you connect with your higher self so that you can communicate with spirit effectively, 'feel' spirit around, heal others, heal yourself, attract what you want into your life in abundance even-anything you ask for. You just need the knowledge and then you have to use it. These principles should be taught to you as you grow, to help understand the power of you as an individual and to fine your direction in life. All to often, the focus is put on academic ability, but what if you are not academic? You may be lucky and have other ideas of a life structure but many children between the ages of 16-20 drift and find that they end up accidently in situations that they previously wouldn't have chosen. Give them the tools necessary, teach them how to use them and they will carve a life. That's not to say that I am referring to academic life being less than it is. With the 2012 prophecy upon us, we are all being swung in a direction that could seem different to the one we had in mind. My mission is to teach you all to have the tools you will require to have in order to live life for a good future and that's not just advice for the children. They will be our inspiration and preparation for what life will bring in the not too distant future. We are all being asked to develop a more spiritual understanding of life. The recession is stripping everything back as people have become too materialistic. We will, however, get the chance to rebuild it all. We have to do this differently though and I think you will agree that it is not before time.

Let's start at base level. Food.

Try and avoid additives. Eat organic where possible. Drink 7-8 glasses of filtered water. Before you have anything to eat in the morning, the liver has been detoxifying overnight. As you get up juice your fruit. Fresh fruit is a great idea as 20 minutes after it is picked/cut it begins to lose its life force and therefore vitamin/mineral quality and benefits to us. Frozen vegetables or fruit. Hmm, well what you've got to think of is would you be any good after being frozen then thawed? Of course not! So where possible, eat as fresh as you can. Home grown is always best. Fresh is next then frozen for full vitamin and mineral quality.

First thing in the morning, juice the fruit of your choice until you have large glass. This should be done before you eat anything. Fruit juice in a carton ferments and is not good for the gut. Drink your juiced fruit and eat nothing until 11 am. This will ensure that the maximum amount of vitamins and minerals are absorbed and they will be processed and will go straight to where they are needed most. You will get headaches for a few days. Drink plenty of water too and after day 4-5 they will pass.

Tea and coffee- Oddly enough, tea is a drink that I see most mediums drink. A few cups a day are beneficial for the system. Tea is a diuretic and although fluid itself, it flushes fluid out of your system also. Tea is a fabulous anti-oxidant so if you drink a cup, try having a glass of water also. Tea should not be too hot before drinking so let it cool for a minute or so. There is evidence that it could be linked to oesophagus cancer if persistently drunk too hot. Coffee is not as healthy to drink. The odd cup is ok but it is generally thought to lower the vibrational level so mediums/healers, do try and avoid this one. If you can't, try a very weak one.

Fizzy drinks are carbonated and effectively you are pumping toxins into your system. Although you get low calorie drink this way, please, it's a big no- no! It will dilute your vibration and encourage your system to struggle as it is like forcing carbonated air into your body, slowing it down with its functions.

IN MODERATION:
Chicken
Fish
Turkey
Beef
Cheese (no additives)
Cream
Milk
Garlic
Eggs

BANNED:

Fizzy drinks

Alcohol

Coffee

Sweets

Chocolate

Sweeteners

Sugar/added

Salt/added

Margarine/low fat spread

Boiled Ham/Bacon/Gammon

Quorn

Fruit juice in Cartons

Lettuce

Any food with additives/pesticides/food dyes, preservatives and white flour are off the agenda also.

ACCEPTABLE FOR YOUR BODY AND VIBRATION:

All fruit except Banana's

All vegetables except Mushrooms

Tofu

Anything from the list of 'Moderation' (in moderation)

Wholemeal bread

Wholemeal pasta

Wholemeal rice

Peanut Butter

Bagels

Yogurts

Whole grain cereals sweetened with fruit

Fructose sugar if you need sugar to sweeten

Remember, Cooking, freezing, canning, micro-waving, steaming, freeze-drying are processes that reduce the life force of your food. Basically anything that would reduce the life force in you will do the same to food. However, it can be hard to eat food in its raw state so steaming gently would be advisable for the foods if there were to be any recommendation at all. I don't want to make it that it is so hard for you to do, the it will put you off.

For supplements, flaxseed oil (you can get them in capsule form also) convert to essential fatty acids you need for good brain function, get rid of the fat in the blood stream, dry skin, excessive thirst (to name but a few), vitamin B6 which help to elevate the serotonin levels and help massively with food cravings (low blood sugar levels) a magnesium, copper, iron and calcium supplement which are essential minerals and vitamins also as today's lifestyle saps these from your system, especially magnesium.

Now, I know you will be sitting there mentally working out how you are going to do all this (that's why I didn't include meal plans in this book) because like I said before, I have not written this to make you stick to an eating plan and then if you can't you feel a failure and you are back to where you started if not in a worse frame of mind. We are spiritually slimming to raise the vibrational level. This newly raised vibration will link with the energy of the universe and you can then ask for what you want and need. Be confident in your capabilities and don't doubt this. We have been fed too much in the way of rubbish and illusion from people who think they know better when it is all down to how the body is and how it responds. I have just sat and listened to someone tell me the they will be happy when they are slimmer, yet I just know that until she explores the whole area of why she is not happy to begin with (remember the whole reasons for the body putting on the weight to begin with) then is it unfair to not address them in your quest for weight loss, for health for well being, for spiritual harmony and balance even> It's like ignoring a friend trying to tell you there's a problem and you carry right on and do what 'you' want to do without listening. You will create more problems and you will then wonder why the weight is going back on or its struggling to release the weight because the mind can't come to terms with what it has experienced.

I used to think it was because the body gets used to dieting but now I think its because you haven't resolved the issues that led to the weight gain in the first place!

*I demolish my bridges behind me...then there is no choice*
*but to move forward.*
(Firdtjof Nansen)

CHAPTER TEN

# EVERY-BODY TELLS A STORY

*Your body is the baggage you must carry through life. The more excess the baggage, the shorter the trip.*
(Arnold H. Glasgow)

What story does your body tell? Is it a sorry tale of sadness, grief, broken hearts, loneliness, anger, resentment, frustration, laziness, desperate and deficit maybe? What are you holding onto or what have you experienced that is holding you back from the very person you should be? Do you like being where you are right now? You are reading this book, and you have made it to chapter ten so I am assuming that you are about to make a change. It takes one day to make a change in your life and today is the day you will make that change. If you don't you will go another year and be in the same place you are now and your vibration will match the feeling of your body and you will still be wondering why nothing fabulous is happening to you and you will hear yourself moan to others and think ' is that me?' I know, as harsh as this sounds, it is true!

I have 'read' for many people over the years, ordinary every day people and famous people alike and when they see me, some of them are desperate and I am a last resort and some of them want a quick fix. It has taken time for you to be in this state and it will take a little bit of time for you to do something about it. But, it takes no time at all to make that decision. Believe it or not, if you are sitting there aware that every day you are moaning over not having enough money, or a slim enough body or you think the boyfriend or girlfriend is cheating on you, you are deciding that you want to stay in that situation and are addicted to moaning about it. There is a saying,

'Shame on them if they do it once but shame on you for allowing them to do it to you a second time'

Meaning, we are supposed to learn by the mistakes we make, but if we are refusing to learn and repeatedly make the same mistakes over and over again, then we are deciding that we are happy making those mistakes. We should never wait for us to hit rock bottom before doing something about our situation but for many of us, it's the wake-up call we need to give us a push. We all have lessons we have to learn also, granted, but how many times can we make that an excuse also? Again, need I remind you that we are still not supposed to repeatedly make those same mistakes, over and over again.

We hide from the truth, choosing to 'deal with it another time when we are ready to do so' and I can accept that. What I struggle with is that even when we are ready, we shy aware and opt for what is familiar or comfortable, don't we?

I have been privileged enough to have met with some amazing people over my life to date and I just know that I will carry on meeting them in the future. I am constantly amazed at the human spirit and what it can withstand and it would put you to shame if you knew of some of the clients I have had the honour of being there for.

I was approached, the other day by a woman who I had coached last year. WOW is the word. I didn't recognise her. She had lost 7 stone!! I told her that she had obviously followed the plan we had made together in our sessions to get structure and control back and had organised her values into some order and I was so pleased to see how she had handled that all superbly! She replied,

'Yes, I thought about it and thought about it and I realised that all the issues I had were leading back to one thing and one thing only, so I dumped the baggage and I found me again. What you see is the result of that and following the food list you gave me. I took the time to make my food sheets up and then forgot about it and just did things to make 'me' happy for a change.'

I was well impressed and so proud of her because I knew what she had gone through before coming to see me. I asked her what she had dumped and she said,

'My husband!'

Well, I nearly fell over-a bit drastic don't you think! However she explained that he had been seeing another woman and she had suspected but he denied it and carried on like nothing was happening. She then dumped him but he left her with £4 in her purse, 6 months unpaid rent on the property and 5 months pregnant with their fourth child! But she focused and now has a beautiful little girl, has moved and has a job she is happy with. She maintains that having her goals helped massively and she stuck to her food choices and hey presto, a **superb seven stone** later, she is happy than she has ever been, free and what she wants, she gets!

Another one of my clients had been to a rock concert last year and had got stuck in the turn styles at the entry point. They had to come and open a door around the side for her to get in. Mortified, she resolved to do something about it and joined a weight loss class. She said that it wasn't enough and realised very quickly that she had to address the very issues that had made her body prone to suffering in this way and she acknowledged loneliness and lack of friendships in her life. She was using food as a friend feeling that she could rely on it more than people. She had to say goodbye to that particular friend as they weren't being very kind to her and make the effort to get out there and make new ones. We came up with some exercises to help her let go and she organised a book group (she loved reading) by putting up posters in the areas she lived and that attracted like minded people to her and she now runs a few of them to help others in the same position she was and has lost just over five stones to date and still going strong. she admits to no longer needing food in her life and she is now in a place that she asked to be. Oh, speaking of her, have just received a phone call right then (probably because I was thinking of her!) and she has just informed me that she has met someone!!! Am so excited for her as she is a lovely person and will be a real asset in any relationship. Well done her!

Another client over the west of Scotland, text me last night to say she has just bumped into the man she wanted to go out with. Now, she talked all the time about this gentleman who kept coming into the shop to chat (he is a policeman) and she had fallen for him. It was obvious that my client needed help. She was giving off the wrong vibes and we needed to change this. There is no point in asking for something until you have the vibrational level right. So we made a plan, I told her to smile and compliment other people. 'Always find something on others to compliment them on. The delight in their voice will make you feel great and as the day goes on your vibrational level will lift and you will feel more and more happy' she did just that and I also said to laugh as she asked (in her mind) for this man to ask her out and the very next day, she went out after work, there he was and he asked her out!! Great work indeed.

I could go on and on telling you these stories, which are uplifting and illuminating. However, I want you to now look at your life, your body, how you feel and then ask yourself if there is something you are willing to do to change all that. Are you a medium in training who just try as you might, can't get the connection right? Are you asking for things like the books tell you to and nothing is happening? Are you trying to lose weight and your body is refusing to drop that weight? Then you need to do something. There is never a right time so do it now. No excuses. You've probably spent your life reacting to circum-stances.

So Pick up that pen and start making that plan. Remember:

Expectations
Values
Goals
Intention
Plan
**Action**

Do you want to look back over your life knowing that you tried or spend your life thinking it was a trial? Trying accomplishes a result in some way, shape or form. If you try with a goal in mind, you will accomplish what you set out to do, and have fun on the way. Let's be happy, ask and receive what we are all capable of being.

Thank you for reading this book.

You are all amazing, wonderful and powerful. If you just but knew it! Well now you do. So what are you waiting for?

Lara xxx

# YOUR ACTION PLAN

# YOUR 'SPIRITUAL SLIMMING' WISH PAGE

# WHAT INSPIRES YOU

# NOTES TO REMEMBER

## 'VIBRATE TO ILLUMINATE'
## YOUR ILLUMINATION PAGES FOR ACHIEVEMENT

**Here write dates, times and moments that you want to mark as being special. Write it as you 'feel it'!**

# 'VIBRATE TO ILLUMINATE'

# 'VIBRATE TO ILLUMINATE'

# BOOKS

MySpiritRadio